Confessio

PIANO PLAYER

An Autobiography

Laurie Holloway

Published 2022
First Edition
NEW HAVEN PUBLISHING LTD
www.newhavenpublishingltd.com
newhavenpublishing@gmail.com

Cover Design © Pete Cunliffe

ISBN: 978-1-912587-71-1

Contents

Foreword – Sir Michael Parkinson 5

Introduction 7

Growing Up 8

Mum and Family 13

What's Coming Up 14

Some Lady Singers 16

Some More Lady Singers 18

Then There Was Dorothy Squires 20

How About Some Male Actors 22

My Early Work 26

Some Male Singers 35

Some More Male Singers 37

Session Work –
and Who Was In Charge 39

Studios 43

Politics 45

Instant Marriage 47

Some More Male Singers 49

When Things Go Wrong 52

Television 55

Some Photos From My Album 64

Golf –
and Other Triumphs and Failures 67

Gordon Mills 75

Gordon Mills Tries Diplomacy 78

Charity and Pastoral Work 80

Some Photos From My Album 84

Some More Lady Singers 86

And Some More Male Singers 89

Clubs, Nightclubs and Theatres 91

John Dankworth and Cleo Laine 93

I Was Judy Garland's Piano Player 96

A Poem by Benny Green 101

Some Personalities 102

Kenny Lynch 104

Radio 106

Dame Edna Everage 107

Some Songwriters 108

Musicians 111

Some Photos From My Album 114

Some Male Actors
(Some Who Sing) 116

Two Bandleaders and
a Musical Polymath 120

HRH Princess Margaret 123

Classical Orchestras 128

Marion 129

From One Subject To Another 130

This Is Your Life 132

Compositions, Publishing
and Recordings 134

Maryann 136

And Finally – My Family Photos 138

The Changing Face of Work
Over the Decades 140

Foreword

L et us get one thing straight from the get-go. Laurie Holloway is a best friend and of that specific group of vagabonds and strolling musicians, he is the man I most admire.

If I have a criticism of my mate it is he makes the difficult look easy as pie. He is not just any old piano player or someone who specialises in one kind of music. His talents range from jazz to classical music working with such diverse talents as Kiri Te Kanawa and Cleo Laine, Stephane Grappelli and Itzhak Perlman.

As a composer he strides with confidence through the widest possible range of music from pop to plainsong. Most admirable of all is that, with all his gifts and international reputation, he remains a lad from Oldham, son of a loving family and the best thing to come out of that doughty Lancashire town apart from the road to Yorkshire.

As a friend he is unfailing and resolute. He is a shrewd observer of his fellow human beings with a patient and consoling attitude for all until he makes his mind up leaving the person he has just met in no doubt if he accepts them or not.

That said, there are many whom he counts as friends, even more who admire his talent and those, myself included, who have spent a lifetime wishing that they could introduce all anecdotes with 'Did I ever tell you about the time I accompanied Princess Margaret?'

On that issue my lips are sealed.

Sir Michael Parkinson

Introduction

I **have had, and I am still having, a wonderful life and career.**

My childhood was very happy and my career has also been more than interesting. I have made many friends, some famous, and some not so famous, but all very interesting. My memories are filled with happiness.

I have had some dark times but there was always light at the end of the tunnel. I have been selfish and at times rather naughty, but I have no regrets.

I hope that you will be entertained by my name dropping stories. I have been associated with famous people, it just happened that way.

Read on, enjoy, have fun, think of me!

Laurie Holloway
Bray 2020

Growing Up

I was born Laurence Holloway, on 31 March 1938 and I come from Oldham in Lancashire, England. I actually wanted to be a tap dancer.

That was my party piece when I was a brat. I'm told I did a fair Fred Astaire when I was about six-years-old, but I didn't pursue this vocation. I decided to be a ballroom dancer instead. I went for weekly lessons to Mr and Mrs MacSweeney. I made some nifty moves on the ballroom floor but I dropped out because I didn't relish dancing with soppy aunts and mums.

Then I became an absolute wizard at roller-skating. All my spare time was spent roaring up and down the schoolyard like a good 'un. During holidays to Scarborough my Mum and Dad would sit in their deck chairs on the beach while I found a skating rink and skated all day long.

Then came my passion for cycling. I can't understand to this day why I have such skinny legs. I'd think nothing of riding my pushbike from my home in Oldham to Morecambe and back in a day – it was about 110 miles and I was only 12-years-old.

I remember Peter Haslam and I went on our bikes to see Oldham Athletic football team play away at Doncaster. That means you go over the Pennines, It was a helluva climb – and it rained all the way home.

We got to a really big climb up to Holmfirth, in Kirklees, West Yorkshire. I was miles away in thought when Peter almost screamed with joy and agony as we got to the top. I had been so far away with my head down that I didn't even know we'd gone up a hill. That's when I first realised there was such a thing as mind over matter!

Me, at about 18 months

We had some good times on our man-powered vehicles – I was a dab hand at tobogganing too. Thinking about it, we really did make our own pleasures. We had a smashing growing-up time. All good lads and healthy exercise.

But, of course, during all this time I was, without realising it, getting quite good at the piano. I never really thought about being a professional musician but, come to think of it, now I realise it was a foregone conclusion.

I started to play the piano when I was four years old. My first piece was "Drink To Me Only With Thine Eyes." I played it in D flat – that is, on all the black notes. I sort of doodled around for the next couple of years and must have impressed the family who, by the way, were all musical.

My first teacher was Mr Emmet who took me on when I was seven. A good teacher, he made sure I had a sound knowledge of theory before he let me touch the piano. He gave me Smallwoods Piano Tutor to cut my teeth on, which I still swear by for any budding John Ogdens.

Every week I used to toddle down a couple of streets to his house and pay my half-a crown for a lesson. This went on for four years and then the day arrived when he said he'd have to ask me not to go again. I was very upset. I presumed I had offended him.

But in actual fact I later learned that he had told my parents I was ready to teach him some tricks!

So, with this background laid by a lovely gentleman, I became organist and choirmaster at the Mission, started playing for dancers instead of being crushed by them – and became something of a freak at school.

At the age of 14 I became semi-pro. I joined the Musicians' Union and was gainfully employed every Saturday night at Billingtons Dance Hall. I think I got 25 bob a night – which was the same money I got two years later for a week as an apprentice draughtsman!

I loved my newfound fame. Lots of kids from school went to Billingtons and when they saw me on stage, well, nothing could stop me.

But the first night of my career was almost a disaster. At the interval the band – well it was a quartet – naturally went to the nearest pub. Me being 14 and a member of a Temperance Mission, I walked to one of my haunts, which was an herbalist where I could get a sarsaparilla. Unfortunately, I didn't have a watch and when I thought it was time to start the second half I toddled back to the hall and almost died when I heard the band playing. They thought I'd called a halt to my hour-old career and gone home.

What a first night!

It was about this time that I started to frequent the Savoy Ballroom. A real big band.

Mum and dad

The Tommy Smith orchestra: trumpets, trombones, saxophones, rhythm section, and two singers. It was terrific. They played all the big band swingers; Tommy had great arrangements done, taken down off the hit records. They sounded even better to me than the originals because it was live.

❄ THE SEARCH FOR A BIG BAND ❄

When I was 14-years-old and playing the piano to about a seven handicap, my ambition was to play in a big band. Not any big band, but the one I considered to be the world's greatest – Tommy Smith's band at the Savoy Ballroom, Oldham. I had yearned to be in the bands of Basie, Ellington, Kenton or Herman, but I didn't need to be in them when Tommy Smith's band could blow them all off the stand. Tommy played all their arrangements anyway, taken down off records, so I didn't need to leave home and Mum's potato pie.

Tommy even had a vocalist who was as good as, if not better than, and certainly identical to Sinatra, Frankie Laine, Johnny Ray and Guy Mitchell. His name was Jackie Allan and today he is still knocking them out in the Blackpool area, and still my good friend. One of his idols was Matt Monroe, and he can sound uncannily like him at times.

But back to my plan! There was one big snag to my ambition... Vernon Jackson!

He was Tommy's piano player. He had been with him for years and looked set for another 20. I so envied him sitting there being part of a wonderful sound that had the Savoy, Oldham, jumping. But my piano-playing handicap was coming down very quickly and I was ready to burst forth, like a butterfly from a chrysalis, onto the breezes of the intoxicating Mulligan and Kenton-filled air.

So I upped and went… away from Mum's delicacies, the Friday night tin bath, my school friends (I was still only 16) and into the venture that I knew was my destiny on the road as a professional musician.

My first job was in a wonderful quartet led by Sid Willmot on baritone sax. He was better than Mulligan! Our bass player, Charlie Aspinall, was famous for having worked in an all-girls band. Bob Wilkinson, the drummer, taught me a new language – drum-speak: gotten-gotten-gotten-giddley-gosh, I was a jazzer. And life was idyllic.

Just as I had planned it. Lie in bed all morning, movies in the afternoon, and play music from 7.30 to 11 in the evening. I ask you. Is that wonderful or not? Full board was three-and-a-half guineas, and if you don't know what three-and-a-half guineas is, well, never mind.

But still I needed to be in a big band. I once called up Mr Ted Heath, who was looking for a new pianist. I had my opening line ready: "May I speak to Mr Heath please?" But he answered the phone himself and I wasn't prepared for that so I hung up, terrified.

I had two years with Joe Daniels and his Hot Shots, which was great foot-tapping fun. We played a season at Bath and a couple of summer seasons at Butlin's holiday camps. I can't call Joe's a big band; it was more of a mainstream jazz line-up, sort of in-between.

At this time the Mecca of jazz was New York. Birdland, on Broadway, was the shrine for any jazz enthusiast, so I decided to go and worship.

I took a job on the Cunard Line as piano player in the ship's band. We travelled from Liverpool to New York every three weeks, playing every kind of music possible: church service, afternoon tea music, bingo cocktail music, dancing every night, and the occasional concert when I did my classical repertoire: very good experience for an 18-year-old.

The ship docked and we would be off to 52nd Street where it was all happening. I discovered that you could pay two dollars fifty cents and sit in Birdland all night and wallow. I wallowed for a year-and-a-half, and then decided to continue my quest for a big band.

❋ FINDING MY FIRST BIG BAND ❋

When I was 21 I at last achieved my ambition. I joined Cyril Stapleton's showband actually 'on the road'. More bliss! It was a very good, if rather polite band. Some wonderful players, still good friends of mine.

I was given a party on the coach returning to London after my first date with the band as a welcome. I was plied with enormous amounts of booze, became totally smashed and fell into a deep sleep.

As a joke, the lads decided not to wake me up when we got to Swiss Cottage in north London where I had left my car – so I was woken by the lady who was cleaning the coach at 6.30 the next morning – in Catford, south London. It was a Sunday; there were no buses. I had no money and was feeling very bad.

I'm still not sure how I got across London to my car but I vaguely remember a lot of milk floats. I told the boys how ill I had felt, how inconvenienced I was, and how rotten they were. They were delighted! I was now a fully-accepted member of the band.

On one return trip from a gig we had one of our frequent 'pit stops' in the middle of nowhere to relieve our bursting bladders. We got back on the coach and waited for a while for one last member, Tony. He didn't return; we went out to look and couldn't find him anywhere. Eventually, we just had to go on.

Some time later we stopped again and Tony climbed down from the roof, laughing his head off at our faces.

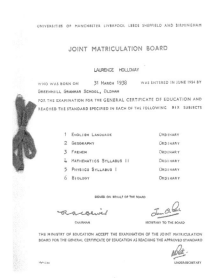

My GCSE Results

An earlier incarnation of Birdland, but now at 315 West 44th Street, New York.

11

Another night our coach driver stopped at traffic lights on the M1. We were horrified and started screaming at him but he said he had to stop because the light was red – he had flipped; he didn't realise he was looking at lights on the adjacent railway line. We decided he should be retired, and that was the end of Jack.

Once, when we did a summer season in Weymouth and I lived in a caravan, my next door neighbour was Ernie Wise. We became – and remained – good friends. One day I had a sudden bout of appendicitis and needed to go to the local hospital, pronto. Ernie was my saviour because he was the only man with a car. To his dying day he told people he was responsible for saving my life! It cost me a few orchestral arrangements. Good value, I'd say!

Now, after a long time in the music business, I am one of perhaps not too many who can say that they got on a Timpsons coach at Swiss Cottage to do a gig somewhere… anywhere; be delivered back sometime in the night, shattered but fulfilled, ready for a fitful morning's sleep before another flight into the hinterland to play foxtrots and quicksteps.

Then the dream ended – abruptly. I became successful!

Success came in the form of freelance session playing. Into the recording studios morning, noon and night; no more lie-ins. In fact, they used to squeeze in 8 am jingles before the 10 o'clock session. No more beloved tangos and waltzes played to a strict metronomic beat. No more movies in daylight hours. Now I was too busy playing on the backing of a conveyor-belt of hits. It was a completely different experience to the one I had visualised as a kid in Oldham.

I later joined John Dankworth's band, but it wasn't on the road. We were resident at a new sophisticated jazz club called the Cool Elephant (where I met an American singer called Marion Montgomery), and later we did seasons at Ronnie Scott's club. No slogging up and down the A1 like itinerant musicians did. The music with John was the most interesting I'd played, but no more seedy digs; no legendary scrubbers like Jean from Leeds who welcomed all visiting bands with open arms (her acrobatics on a glass-topped table are well documented in many a brass player's memory); no more exhausting overnight treks to Cornwall, followed by Aberdeen, then Bournemouth.

Still, I had done it with Cyril. And I'm pleased I had. Pity I didn't get to play with Tommy Smith and those great Billy May charts, though I do play them still – in my head.

Thanks, Tommy, for inspiring me, and pointing me in the right direction.

❋ PETS ❋

Aunty Doris's husband was dear Uncle Harold.

They used to house and dog-sit when Marion and I were away. Our dog was Sugar, a lovely Yorky.

One year we were visiting friends in Hopfgarten, a village in Austria. I thought that I should call home to see if everything was alright. Uncle Harold answered the phone and told me that Sugar, our dog, wasn't well.

I asked him what was wrong and he said "She's dead."

I suppose he didn't want to tell us the sad news straight away, so he broke it gently.

❋ MUM AND FAMILY ❋

My dear mother had two sisters, my Aunty Doris and my Aunty Ada. They spent quite a lot of time at my house in Bray.

One year I was the musical director of the Terry Wogan show – a live television show on New Year's Eve from the Television Centre at White City in London. This meant that I couldn't be at our own New Year's Eve party at Elgin... The house guests on that particular New Year's Eve included the highly successful composer, Cy Coleman. He wrote many wonderful songs such as "I've Got Your Number" and "Real Live Girl", "Sweet Charity", "Big Spender" and "If My Friends Could See Me Now".

Cy Coleman,
14 June 1929 – 8 November 2004.
Songwriters Hall of Fame

Late in the evening he regaled my family and guests with a selection of his famous songs, playing them on the piano. While he was playing, my car was seen to arrive home. Aunty Doris, who didn't have a clue who Mr Coleman was, said "You can stop now Cy, our Laurie's here!"

❋ ❋❋❋❋❋❋❋❋❋❋❋❋❋❋❋❋

Aunty Ada, Aunty Doris and my mother unexpectedly came into a small amount of inheritance. I asked them why they had benefited from this windfall. Aunty Doris told me that a distant relative who they didn't know had left the funds to them.

Aunty Doris said that she had died intestate. Aunty Ada said that was wrong, she had died in Cyprus!

❋ THE MISSION ❋

As mentioned, when I was 14 years old in 1952, I became the organist and choirmaster at my local church, George Johnson's Gospel Temperance Mission. I played an old organ which I had to inflate with my knees, I suppose they were bellows.

I used to go to the Mission twice each Sunday. Firstly, to the afternoon children's school and the serious one in the evening which was a proper service with a guest speaker each week.

My Aunty Doris was a Sunday school teacher and she suggested that I sign the teetotal pledge. I did. Many years later I probably disappointed her by starting to have the odd alcoholic drink. Sorry Aunty Doris.

We weren't high church. We were called "free church". For me it was a brilliant chance to learn the hymns and the four-part writing: Soprano, Alto, Tenor and Bass. Good grounding for future projects. I was paid £1 per week. Quite a sum for a young lad. During the week, my friends, Peter Haslam and my cousin Winston Hughes and I would go to the Mission to play table tennis. I became quite good at it, and Peter and I were picked for the Oldham team. We played Manchester. We lost heavily. We weren't picked again.

One night we were practising, and we suddenly discovered smoke coming out of the loft. It was an electrical fire. It's a good job we were there. I went up into the loft and somehow put out the fire. I was a hero. My trousers were ruined so the committee bought me a new pair. Our lives centred around the Mission. It was a good base for my future life.

WHAT'S COMING UP -
NAME DROPPING

Allan Ganley on drums and Ken Baldock on bass were with me as the rhythm section for John Dankworth and Cleo Laine.

Ken was a very good bass player but also the buffoon of the group.

I remember that once we performed at Dynevor Castle and were greeted at the entrance by Lord Dynevor himself. Ken thought he was a servant and got him to carry his bags. How embarrassing.

Keith Christie was a tremendous jazz trombonist. We shared a dodgy glass of wine once, and he said that the grape was probably from the shady side of the chateau.

I worked at the upmarket Gargoyle Club in Meard Street, Soho for two years. I accompanied lots of great lady jazz singers. I remember playing for Beryl Bryden, Adelaide Hall and Dinah Washington. Good memories.

Johnny Harris was with me in the Cyril Stapleton Orchestra. He was a fine trumpet player and arranger. I worked with him a lot at the Pye studios near Marble Arch because he was Tony Hatch's chief arranger. He arranged lots of songs for Petula Clarke.

I was the musical director for Canon and Ball when they did their first show, for Southern Television.

I was the pianist, arranger and friend of Val Doonican (we jokingly called him Vile Hooligan) for many years of television and albums.

I was the pianist for the American song writer Sammy Cahn. He and I travelled extensively to perform his one-man show.

I was the musical director for Freddie Starr's *Variety Madhouse*. At the end of one show he asked me to carry on playing. Little did I know that he was going to pour a bucket of joke soap over my head. I got a new dress suit because of it.

Val Doonican,
3 February 1927 – 1 July 2015.

Russ Abbot was one of the cast and he had his own series later. I was his musical director. Russ and I met up often on Barbados where he spends the winter. Very sensible.

Over the years I have played on *Music While You Work* with Harry Leader, and *Workers' Playtime*, a live lunchtime radio broadcast.

I did a tribute with the jazz trumpet player, Dizzy Gillespie.

I have been a friend of the Doncaster diva, Lesley Garrett, for many years. I have been pleased to be featured on her television show.

I performed with Michael Crawford on television shows as his pianist.

I was interviewed by Aled Jones for a Welsh programme similar to *Desert Island Discs*. He and I also met up on *Strictly* when I was the musical director and he was a celebrity dancer.

I have been a friend of Gloria Hunniford for ages. I did her television show a long time ago and we often bump into each other.

My late wife, Marion Montogomery, and I were invited to the home of Claire and Des Rayner for lunch. We found out the reason when photographers were involved in taking photos of us for a gourmet magazine.

Robin Douglas Home and I wrote a terrible song together. He had written the lyric for a song called "Blue Birthday".

He had been rather friendly with Princess Margaret and she had given him the brush off. He was somewhat distraught.

I could go on, mentioning lots of people with whom I have been associated, but I think that is enough for now.

Did I tell you that I was the subject of *This Is Your Life*? That I got an MBE from the Queen?

And that I reminded her that I played the piano at Buckingham Palace for Her Majesty and Princess Margaret?

Maybe I *should* mention some more names that I have worked with or met: Eddie Grant (the DJ), Graham Norton with Liza Minnelli, Don Black the lyricist, Elizabeth Taylor, Ella Fitzgerald, Englebert Humperdink and Judy Garland. Tommy Blaize (one of my singers on Strictly), Jacqui Dankworth (to whom I am virtually an uncle).

I played on the *Parkinson* show for Robbie Williams, Sacha Distel and many other names.

Martin Taylor the wonderful guitarist is a very good friend.

Enough, enough, I hear you say. Let's get on with the book!

With Aled Jones.

Some Lady Singers

THE THREE DAMES

I was asked to be the musical director of a fantastic project. It was called "The Three Dames".

It was just after the three tenors had been so successful.

They were all honoured by the Queen with a Damehood. Their names were Dame Kiri Te Kanawa, Dame Shirley Bassey and Dame Cleo Laine.

Fabulous.

I rehearsed each Dame, and everything was going swimmingly. The idea was to mix and match. For example. Kiri would sing jazz standards, Cleo would sing something classical, and Shirley, well she would sing whatever she wanted to sing.

I went to Kiri's house and we rehearsed. I went to Cleo's house and we rehearsed. I went to Shirley in Monte Carlo and rehearsed "Send In The Clowns" She was fantastic!

So, everything was ready for the production.

Then the phone call. "It's off." I asked why such a fantastic project would stall at the last minute. I was told that one of them wanted more than a third!

You can imagine what the other two said.

I suggested that we replace the odd one out with Dame Edna. Not appreciated.

So ended a very good idea. Greed raised its ugly head.

THE THREE DEGREES

I was the conductor for Engelbert Humperdinck for five years. We carried a rhythm section, a valet, a road manager, a hairdresser and lots of hangers-on. You'll read more about that later.

The show was opened by a singing group who later became our backing singers. Each year it was a different group.

We had a group called Celebration. One called The Promises. I remember a group from Mussel Shoals.

One year it was The Three Degrees – Sheila, Fayette and Valerie. They were very good. They had a record out which became a big hit: "When Will I See You Again".

Amazingly, Sheila came to live in Bray, across the road from me. She had married a local gentleman. She had a couple of children by him and everything was dandy.

One day, to my great surprise, Valerie, who I hadn't seen for a few years, walked up my road pushing a pram.

I was relieved to find that the child within the pram belonged to Sheila.

It was good to see Valerie again.

JUDY JONES

When I met and played for Marion, I was at the time living with another singer called Judy Jones.

She had been the singer with the Cyril Stapleton Band when I was the pianist. I knew that she was older than me and one day I saw her passport. I was 24 and she was 36.

Perfect for a young stud! But two things happened.

I met Marion, and I thought that when I was 59 years old Judy would be 71.

Not so clever.

I left Judy and concentrated on Marion. Judy sued me for breach of promise. It was still around at that time. I was threatened with court action but Judy dropped it before it went to court. End of an interesting episode!

✳ ✳✳✳✳✳✳✳✳✳✳✳✳✳✳✳✳✳✳

Jazz singer weds Oldham pianist

AFTER a two-month show-business romance, Laurie Holloway, an Oldham pianist, married Marian Montgomery, the American jazz singer, in Gainesville, Georgia, yesterday.

Laurie, whose parents live in Trafalgar Street, Oldham, met Marian when she came to Britain to top the bill at London's Cool Elephant Club for two weeks. He was a member of Johnny Dankworth's band accompanying the singer. The couple fell in love and became engaged.

Before returning to America at the end of her club engagement, Marian starred in her own show on ITV, and appeared twice on the Eamonn Andrews Show, when she was accompanied by Laurie.

Laurie followed her to America three weeks later, when the Dankworth band ended its season at the Cool Elephant.

Back in July

Laurie, who is 27, was a professional musician when he was 16. He has since played with many "name" bands, including those of Cyril Stapleton and Johnnie Gray. He has also accompanied Judy Garland, Cleo Laine, Anthony Newley and Marion Ryan.

His parents, Mr. and Mrs. Marcus Holloway, said today they had never met Miss Montgomery. They received an invitation to the wedding, but decided it was too far to travel.

"We are looking forward to meeting her in July," said Mrs. Holloway. "They are hoping to get back to Britain then."

"We understand they are honeymooning in New Orleans," she said

MARION MONTGOMERY

Headline news, but with a typo on the second line.

Some More Lady Singers

❋ ❋❋❋❋❋❋❋❋❋❋❋❋❋❋❋❋❋

ELLA FITZGERALD

Ella Fitzgerald,
25 April 1917 – 15 June 1996.

I was the piano player in the Johnny Spence orchestra at the BBC, for a television special featuring the wonderful Ella Fitzgerald.

The orchestra was littered with super- star musicians. Tubby Hayes, Don Lusher, etc.

She also did part of the show with her own trio – The Tommy Flanagan Trio.

One of Ella's most famous songs is "Manhattan". The verse to "Manhattan" was just piano and voice.

I will never ever forget being Ella's accompanist for those 8 bars.

I even have the video to prove it! Another indelible memory.

I met Ella once more when I was a guest on the Oscar Peterson television series.

I didn't play for her then because Oscar did!

❋ ❋❋❋❋❋❋❋❋❋❋❋❋❋❋❋❋

ODETTA

"There's a hole in the bucket, dear Liza, dear Liza,

There's a hole in the bucket, dear Liza, a hole.

Well, fix it, dear Henry, dear Henry, dear Henry,

Well, fix it, dear Henry, dear Henry, fix it."

These words were sung in that well- known song by Odetta and Harry Belafonte.

She was an American singer. She was a rather large black lady.

I was booked by the great trumpet player Kenny Baker, to play for Odetta at the Savoy Theatre for a week. The only musician she brought with her was her bass player.

After a couple of nights the bass player told me that Odetta digged me.

I said that I was very pleased that she liked my piano playing.

He said "No man. She digs you." I was single at the time.

Enough said!

❋ ❋❋❋❋❋❋❋❋❋❋❋❋❋❋❋❋

VERA LYNN

Dame Vera Margaret Lynn CH DBE OStJ, 20 March 1917 – 18 June 2020.

In 1995 there were celebrations for the 50th anniversary of the end of the War. I was asked to be the musical director of a television show on the QE2. We sailed from Southampton to Cherbourg.

On the show were many celebrities. Dame Vera Lynn was the main guest.

I went to her house and we rehearsed the songs for the show. Her usual wartime hits of course.

She asked me if I would like a cup of tea and I said yes please, "I take it with milk and two sugars." She was horrified by my request for two sugars. She then gave me my tea and said that I was to try it without any sugar at all. It tasted revolting to me.

She then put in one spoonful of sugar and told me to try it. It tasted so much better. She said "There you are. I've cut your sugar consumption down by a half already!"

I have learned, thanks to Dame Vera, to take my tea without any sugar at all.

❊ ❊❊❊❊❊❊❊❊❊❊❊❊❊❊❊❊❊

DIANA DORS

I was the musical director of a television series featuring Diana Dors. I wrote the signature tune. It was called "Spend Some Time With Me". What happened to it, I don't know.

❊ ❊❊❊❊❊❊❊❊❊❊❊❊❊❊❊❊❊

TINA MAY

Tina May is one of my favourite people. She also happens to be one of my favourite singers. I have known her for many years. She and I do a show where I name drop, a bit like this book, and she sings relative songs.

We have done the show at various nightclubs and we both support the Actors' club in Covent Garden. We have done several shows there, charitably, for the elderly retired actors who frequent it. Me included.

We have also made a CD, *Happy Memories*, where we have recorded songs which mean something to us.

I am involved in a music trust and we hold a seminar every year. Tina has been a wonderful tutor to the young aspiring students. What more can I say? She is a good friend and my wife and I like her a lot.

Since I wrote my memoirs Tina has died. I believe that she had a brain tumour. I was surprised and devastated and I had no idea that she was ill. She never mentioned it to me.

Tina and I made the album *Happy Memories*. Just Tina and me. An apt title, because I will always have Happy Memories of her.

❊ ❊❊❊❊❊❊❊❊❊❊❊❊❊❊❊❊❊

Then There Was Dorothy Squires

❄ ❄❄❄❄❄❄❄❄❄❄❄❄❄❄❄❄❄

TOMMY SANDERSON

I lived in a caravan in a car park in Haringey. I had been in London for about a year and my name was beginning to get around.

Pinterest

With second husband Roger Moore,
Dorothy Squires, 25 March 1915 – 14 April 1998.

Sir Roger Moore, 14 October 1927 – 23 May 2017.

Dorothy had as her accompanist a lovely man called Tommy Sanderson. I had met him a few times and he had heard me play, so he knew my capabilities.

One night the communal phone rang and everybody rushed out to see if it was for them. The caravan site was inhabited by out-of-work artists and musicians. It turned out that this time it was for me! Tommy Sanderson was stuck in fog on the M1 and couldn't possibly get down to London from Birmingham in time to do the club in Berkeley Square, with Dorothy. Would you please deputise for him?

I was absolutely thrilled! My first taste of the big time in accompanying a big star. I arrived at the club and asked to be shown to Miss Squire's dressing room.

I was duly shown down some stairs to a corridor and told that the door in front of me was "the room of Miss Squires."

I knocked on the door and a lady's voice told me to enter. This was it! Stardom!

I was alone with Miss Squires and told her that my name was Laurie Holloway, and that I had had a call from Tommy to say that he was stuck in fog and couldn't make it tonight.

Her gentle remark was – "Tommy can't f***ing make it?"

My bubble burst.

This was my introduction to the big time. Shattered as I was I went on and did the show. I think she was pleased. I didn't hang around very long at the end of the show.

Dorothy was my neighbour and we met several times since our first soirée, but I'm convinced that she didn't recall our first conversation.

Lovely lady.

❄ ❄❄❄❄❄❄❄❄❄❄❄❄❄❄❄❄❄

DORIS GARD

Dorothy was a highly paid and highly successful singer of the 1940s and early '50s.

She was that period's Shirley Bassey. She topped the bill wherever she went and made a fortune doing it. A gentleman called Nicky Welsh who also lived on the caravan site was her musical director. Her band drank for England and were very unruly.

One night she introduced her orchestra and said that they were all fired. That was Dorothy.

Many years later, I moved into my present house and Dorothy lived across the road. We became very friendly. She was by this time past her sell-by date and I presume had spent her small fortune on suing people. She sued everybody, including her ex-husband, Roger Moore.

Whenever she visited our house, she asked me if I would play the piano for her when she performed at Carnegie Hall in New York. I said that I would, knowing that it would never happen. It didn't.

Dorothy had a secretary and companion named Doris Gard.

In one of her frightening tantrums, Dorothy threw Doris out one night and Doris came to our house for somewhere to spend the night. Late on this hot summer's night the phone rang next to my bed. It was Dorothy. She said "Is that f***ing woman with you?"

I immediately told Marion, my wife, that it was a call for her. I was chicken.

Marion, in her deep-south American drawl, told Dorothy to mind her language and that we would speak tomorrow. The bedroom balcony doors were open because of the heat. Dorothy appeared in the street and yelled "You can put the f***ing phone down but I can still shout at you."

The next day Doris went back to Dorothy. I later told Roger Moore this story, he was interested but he said that he wasn't surprised.

Dorothy eventually went to a nursing home in Wales because she was ill and broke. Sadly, she died there. A tremendous character who had lived life to the full.

RIP Dorothy Squires.

Elizabeth Taylor

ELIZABETH TAYLOR AND STEVEN SONDHEIM

I was the pianist on the film *A Little Night Music* by Stephen Sondheim.

Mr Sondheim asked me if I would stay behind after one session to help Elizabeth Taylor to learn to sing "Send In The Clowns". She was gorgeous.

In the small studio were Stephen Sondheim, Elizabeth Taylor, Jonathon Tunick the arranger and conductor, and me.

All started well. Miss Taylor got the first bit right.

Then the trouble started. She couldn't get the middle section right.

The conductor Jonathon Tunick said that when we reached the middle section, he would point out the melody on the cellos.

Elizabeth said, "Dear boy, you'll have to point out the f***ing cellos."

I fell on the floor, laughing.

How About Some Male Actors

❇ ❇❇❇❇❇❇❇❇❇❇❇❇❇❇❇❇❇

STEWART GRANGER

IMDb

Stewart Granger, 6 May 1913 – 16 August 1993.

I was in my local hostelry having dinner with the American film star Stewart Granger, Michael and Mary Parkinson, Jimmy and Pauline Tarbuck and my wife Marion Montgomery.

Stewart had recently been a guest of Michael Parkinson on his talk show.

We had a splendid dinner and Jimmy Tarbuck was his usual hilarious self and was making us laugh as he always does.

Marion's back was near the window ledge and along it there were lighted candles.

Marion had lacquer on her hair and when Jimmy said something hilarious, she leaned back, and her hair touched a candle and set it on fire.

Stewart Granger, the swashbuckling hero of many a film, froze, and squealed in a high pitched voice.

Jimmy was close to Marion and calmly threw a napkin over her hair and extinguished the fire.

❇❇❇❇❇

I changed my opinion of the daredevil Stewart Granger from that moment. He was brilliant on film, but in real life… well, my eyes were opened.

❇ ❇❇❇❇❇❇❇❇❇❇❇❇❇❇❇❇❇

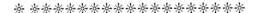

CLINT EASTWOOD

When in Las Vegas with Engelbert Humperdinck, I often played golf with Buddy Greco, the singer and pianist.

At the time he was married to Dani, a beautiful lady.

My wife and I became good friends with her and Buddy. We were invited to a party at her apartment in Los Angeles.

Wikipedia

Clint Eastwood

I knocked on the door and it was opened by none other than Edward G. Robinson.

Very impressive. He probably did that everywhere, for effect.

Dani and Buddy eventually divorced. She moved on to the actor who played The Fugitive, David Janssen. They married in 1975 and remained together until Janssen's death.

❄ ❄❄❄❄

My wife, Marion and I were booked to play Shelley's Manhole, a club in Los Angeles.

We invited Dani to see us and she turned up with Clint Eastwood. Horace Silver, the great pianist was in the audience.

I was in a predicament. I wanted to say Hello to Horace and I wanted to say Hello to Clint Eastwood. I decided to have a chat with Horace. He was lovely. Pianist to Pianist. But I was keen to go to the dressing room and see Clint, so I did. I was talking to Clint and I was told that the interval was finished.

I complained that I was having a wonderful, meaningful conversation with my mate Clint.

Not impressed, I had to go on and play for Marion.

❄❄❄❄❄

Fast forward many years – I was the musical director of the Parkinson show.

The guest one week was Clint Eastwood. I reminded him of our meeting in Los Angeles.

I asked him if he still saw Dani Greco . He said that he saw her occasionally.

I'll bet he did.

✳ ✳✳✳✳✳✳✳✳✳✳✳✳✳✳✳✳✳

JOHNNY WEISMULLER

Johnny Weismuller

I was conducting for Engelbert Humperdinck in Las Vegas and was about to return home and went to the airport.

In the waiting room was Johnny Weismuller, better known as Tarzan. He actually had been a world champion swimmer.

My good friend Harry Paton Evans has a son who was Tarzan mad.

So I went up to Tarzan and asked if he would kindly sign his autograph for Stuart.

He invited me to sit down next to him and we had a chat.

He told me that he lived in Las Vegas (we called it Lost Wages) and I told him that I had been Humperdinck-ing.

A lovely chat for a while and then his flight was called. We shook hands and said our goodbyes.

At the door he turned around and said "Just for you Laurie," and he did his Tarzan yell.

Wow, Tarzan yelled for me! Another amazing memory.

✳ ✳✳✳✳✳✳✳✳✳✳✳✳✳✳✳✳✳

✳ ✳✳✳✳✳✳✳✳✳✳✳✳✳✳✳✳✳✳✳

RONNIE BARKER

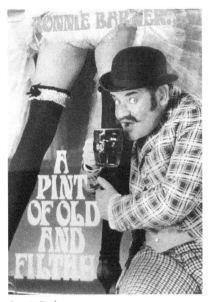

Ronnie Barker

I met Ronnie Barker when I was doing the David Frost show and Ronnie was a regular guest. We became good friends.

We did a weekly television series that was led by David Frost. Ronnie did lots of comedy sketches with Ronnie Corbett.

Nearly every week, sketches were sent in by a gentleman called Gerald Wiley. Most of them were funny and they were used in the show.

He never made an appearance, he just sent the sketches in every week.

At the end of the series, in gratitude for using his material, he invited some of the cast, including me, to dinner at a restaurant nearby. A place was reserved for the mysterious Gerald Wiley.

When he didn't show up and there had been an uncomfortable wait, up got Ronnie Barker to say that he was the phantom Gerald Wiley.

Wow. He had rejected some sketches, so we were convinced that he wasn't Gerald Wiley.

A very clever Barkerism.

He told me that he had written some lyrics and wondered if I would complete his project by writing the music, arranging it for a pseudo pit band, and taking care of the musicians and the recording session. Quite a project for me. Of course, I agreed.

It started in January and I composed the music and directed the band at the end of February. Quite fast. The band consisted of my usual musicians. Kenny Baker, Don Lusher, Ray Swinfield, Judd Proctor, Dave Richmond and Alf Bigden. Me on piano and Musical Director.

The album is quite rude. Full of double entendres. It's called A Pint Of Old And Filthy. It cemented the relationship between Ronnie and me. Every year Ronnie and his wife Joy held a summer party at their house, and Marion and I were always invited.

I don't think the album was a big seller, but I do get the odd fourpence halfpenny when it's played on the radio. Mainly in Scandinavia for some reason.

Ronnie dropped the bombshell that he was retiring in 1987 and opened an antique shop with Joy, his dear wife.

In 2007 his health deteriorated and he died aged 77 in 2008. A lovely man and very talented. There was a memorial at Westminster

Abbey and instead of the usual two, there were "Four Candles".

✳ ✳✳✳✳✳✳✳✳✳✳✳✳✳✳✳✳✳✳

MY EARLY WORK

❋ ❋❋❋❋❋❋❋❋❋❋❋❋❋❋❋❋❋❋❋

THE *CARINTHIA*

Arthur Plant played the alto saxophone. He had a very good band at the Palais in Dundee.

I joined the band in 1955. We played great music; in fact, we were eventually fired because the music was great but not the best for dancing. After all, it was a ballroom for dancing.

The band comprised Harry Hall on trumpet, a really good player, Arthur on saxophone and clarinet, three more saxophones whose names I forget, me on piano, and Eddie Hopkins on bass and Eddie Hopkins on drums. Two gentlemen with the same name, different instruments. It was a good band.

I rented a flat with my lady friend, Julie Macdonald, and we married on my 18th birthday.

We had our daughter, Karon Julie, nine months and nine days later. Everything was pretty good.

Arthur and I auditioned in Edinburgh for Mr Gerald Bright (Geraldo), who was the musical boss and employer for the Cunard shipping line. The musicians were known as Geraldo's Navy.

We got a job on the maiden voyage of the RMS *Carinthia*. Our route was Liverpool to Montreal via Quebec, in the summertime, and to New York in the winter when the St Lawrence froze over.

That's the bit I liked. Birdland jazz club was my home address in New York.

We did a five day crossing and three days off at each end of the trip. I really enjoyed New York.

RMS Carinthia was an ocean liner built in 1956 as one of the four Saxonia class ships.

WEST INDIES CHRISTMAS AND NEW YEAR'S CRUISE

CUNARD  LINE

R.M.S. "CARINTHIA"

Captain D. M. MacLean, D.S.C., R.D., R.N.R.
Cruise Director : Mr. Herman Holtberg

CONCERT by ANDREA ZANNIS
BARITONE

Accompanied at the Piano by NORMAN MARTIN

in the PROMENADE DECK LOUNGE

at 9.45 p.m. tonight, Friday, December 28, 1956

Orchestral Selections by

ARTHUR PLANT and his "CARINTHIA" ORCHESTRA
Presented by Geraldo of London

Artists provided by

NAT M. ABRAMSON, 1440 Broadway, New York City

Overture ... ... "Carousel"	*Rodgers & Hammerstein*
"Tristesse"	*...F. Chopin*
"Eri Tu Che Macchiavi"	*...G. Verdi*
Aria from Opera "Un Ballo in Maschera"	
Piano Solo ... ..."Moonlight Sonata" ...	*...Beethoven*
LAURIE HOLLOWAY	
"You'll Never Walk Alone"	*Rodgers & Hammerstein*
"Largo Al Factotum"	*...Rossini*
Aria from "Il Barbiere di Siviglia"	
Selection ... ... "Firefly"	*Friml*

We also did a Caribbean cruise from New York. It was fantastic. Remember I was only 18 years old. I shared a cabin with my good friend, the tenor saxophone player, Bill Robinson. I had the top bunk.

One of the stewards was someone I didn't meet until much later. He lived below decks and I was up in the posh end. His name was John Prescott, now Lord Prescott. He and his wife, Pauline, are good friends of mine. Strange world.

The playing was extremely varied. A normal day started with tea music. We played for the passengers as they sipped their tea and ate their cakes. Arthur put away his saxophone and played his violin. We played lots of medleys from the most famous musicals. Carousel, Oklahoma, etcetera.

I remember that it was the first time that I had played West Side Story. Brilliant.

After dinner I played solo piano for the people to play Bingo - I played in between games.

Then we played for dancing. Starting after the Bingo, we played until the early hours of the morning. The only deviation of that routine was on a Sunday when we played hymns for the church service.

If the end of Saturday night dancing and the start of the church service on Sunday morning was less than eight hours, we got extra money. Not much but every little helped.

I did a year on the Carinthia and enjoyed every minute.

But it was time to move on.

✻ NAPPIES ✻

After my year on the Carinthia, I auditioned at the Midland Hotel in Manchester for a job with their company which was owned by British Rail. I played in the small group, like the Max Jaffa ensemble. Quite classical.

I passed the audition and was offered the job playing the piano at another British Rail hotel, Gleneagles. If I had played golf at the time I would have jumped at the offer, but I didn't until later, so I turned it down.

I went to join the Joe Daniels band in 1958. We did a season in Bath, Somerset and I enjoyed playing the happy music of what was known as "mainstream jazz".

I did an arrangement each week, and wrote it out for the musicians, for which I got paid an extra £1.

We lived in a very cold flat above a newsagent. My wife, Julie, took a job in a grocery store, and I baby-sat my daughter Karon during the day.

I was a dab hand at changing nappies. Karon was only a year old.

After Bath we went to Butlin's camps in the summer.

We did a season at Skegness which was very interesting to me as that is where I was conceived in 1937.

I wondered in which chalet my parents had been intimate. I believe it was the start of mixed bathing that had been the culprit.

It was a happy band and happy innocent times with Joe Daniels.

Again, time to move on.

MY EARLY WORK

❋ ❋❋❋❋❋❋❋❋❋❋❋❋❋❋❋❋❋❋❋❋❋

My first band - Sid Willmot.

LES MOSS (1955)

I've just remembered. I went to Sheffield Locarno on New Year's Eve, 1956 to play the piano in the Les Moss band. I considered myself a seriously good musician.

I got to the Locarno and saw that it was "Crazy Week". Not my cup of tea. I played the first night and immediately put in my notice. I wanted to get out of this band as quickly as possible. Les Moss was not amused. He became quite belligerent and said some nasty things to me.

I was only 17 years old and this was the first disappointment of my career. Well the second if we count being fired on New Year's Eve by Sid Willmot. I was glad to get away and went on my way to Dundee to join a "proper" band – Arthur Plant's.

With the Sid Willmot Rythm Section.

With the Arthur Plant Band

❋ ❋❋❋❋❋❋❋❋❋❋❋❋❋❋❋❋❋❋

HARINGEY

When I was 20 years old I lived, as previously mentioned, in a caravan at Haringey, North London. I was married to Julie and my daughter was Karon.

I was full of myself. I had managed to get the job as pianist in the Ronnie Rand Ballroom Orchestra at the Astoria Charing Cross Road.

The hours were 2.30 till 6 pm and 7.30 to 10.30 pm. There were two bands with the famous revolving bandstand.

I was asked to be the pianist with Alan Kane at the Gargoyle club in Meard Street. The Gargoyle club job started at 10.30 pm.

Fortunately the Astoria Charing Cross Road clock was five minutes fast. So I accepted the job. That meant that I worked from 2.30 till 6.00, 7.30 to 10.25, and 10.30 to 3.15 am.

Quite a long day.

I was driving an Austin big seven at the time. It broke down one day and that was the end of it because it was as old as me, born in 1938.

I learned a lot of tunes because I was playing the piano for 13 hours a day. In the breaks I would go to a jazz club called the Downbeat Club in Old Compton Street. Never enough music.

I continued in this fashion for two years. I was in my element because I was playing music.

Sadly, I neglected my home life, my family, and my daughter Karon.

I was very selfish and blinkered.
Fortunately after many, many years I am reconciled with my first family.

With first wife Julie and daughter Karon at a happy occassion.

THE GARGOYLE AND THE ASTORIA

Talking about the Gargoyle reminds me of the time I fell madly in love with a stripper. She was beautiful. 18 years old, lovely face and a figure that was deserving of a standing ovation.

I always gave her one (a standing ovation).

I spent hours of my time trying to persuade her that this was not the life for her. How could she take off her clothes and display her tender, lithe, young body to all those lecherous old sods? How could she share her nudity with all those horrid, sordid, rich idiots when it should have been for my eyes alone.

All to no avail! She jilted me and started living with the owner of the club.

Complete disillusionment.

I later took my wife, Marion, to the club (she was dying to see what I had been up to) and there was Janet, still in the buff, but looking like a really seedy Danny La Rue. I wonder where she is now...?

At this time I was "doubling" the Astoria, Charing Cross Road, with the Gargoyle. My work at the Astoria finished at 10.30 pm and I started at the Gargoyle at 10.30 pm.

I achieved this slight of hand by having the clock at the Astoria being five minutes fast.

I would dash off the stage and roar round the corners of streets – Greek, Frith and Dean and have the tiny elevator held waiting for me by the helpful doorman. Up I'd go, quick change of jacket, sit down, and straight into the chorus of "La Mer" with a quarter bottle of scotch tucked in my pocket which was usually gone by the time we got to "A Foggy Day In London Town".

On the way to the club I would shout a greeting to my friends the prostitutes, who in those days adorned every doorway. They knew my vocation and would shout "Hurry up Laurie, you're a bit late tonight!"

✳ ✳✳✳✳✳✳✳✳✳✳✳✳✳✳✳✳✳

JOHNNY GRAY

Johnny Gray had the band at the Hammersmith Palais every Sunday. I was the pianist. I was aged about 20. We met in the pub next door – the Laurie Arms, at 7 pm when they opened.

We drank for England. I was regularly sick before we went on stage at 7.30 pm.

Again, always with Johnny Gray, we had a great time. The band was called Johnny Gray and His Band of the Day. We called it "Johnny Gray and his band of DECAY".

We also had a weekly gig at the Savoy Ballroom, Catford. The place was always heaving. Johnny would say things like "Get your birds in for the weekend."

And "Change your partners, change your luck."

Very rude, but just right for the atmosphere.

Wikipedia

Johnny Gray, 15 May 1920 – 17 June 2014.

THE CATSKILLS WITH JOHNNY GRAY

Picclick

Terry Burton, 1936? - October 2018.

The Musicians' Union decided that to allow American Musicians to work in the UK, the same number of musicians would go to work in the USA.

Dave Brubeck was booked to work in the UK so a similar number of British Musicians' Union members would be booked to go to the USA, wanted or not.

Jonny Gray was not wanted but his quartet were booked to play The Pines Hotel in the Catskills, New York. I was the pianist. We had a wonderful time.

I became known as "Slolly 'olloway" because every night Johnny had had a few whiskies and found it difficult to say Laurie Holloway.

There was an ice-skating rink and I spent a lot of time on there.

Our singer was Terry Burton, a very good singer of Doris Day songs. Also very attractive. (I was single, enough said.)

Dave Brubeck was a great success in the UK but I bet he didn't have as much fun as we did in the Catskills.

❋ ❋❋❋❋❋❋❋❋❋❋❋❋❋❋❋❋❋

CYRIL STAPLETON

(We affectionately called him "Sterile Simpleton".)

As mentioned, I was very busy playing the piano at the Astoria and the Gargoyle club.

I had Sundays off, until I took the gig at the Manor House pub with the Mike Senn band, every Sunday evening. No wonder my marriage didn't last.

The drummer at the Manor House pub was Paul Brodie. He was also the drummer with Cyril Stapleton. Cyril had what we called a Name Band.

That was a famous band that featured on television and did touring dates.

His pianist had been the wonderful Bill McGuffie. The present pianist was Don Innes and he was leaving to go somewhere else. I auditioned at the Porchester Hall and Cyril invited me to join his well-known orchestra. I felt elated and I believed that I was on the way to notoriety.

We did a television series called *The Melody Dances* from the Finsbury Park Empire. One week I was featured playing a solo. Johnny Harris arranged "Fascinating Rhythm" for me to play.

My brother Marcus came along to support me. I needed it because I was physically sick with nerves before the show.

The orchestra did trips all over the country to ballrooms as a Name Band. The first one I did was to Looe in Cornwall. Quite a journey.

✳ ✳✳✳✳✳✳✳✳✳✳✳✳✳✳✳✳✳✳

A SIGN OF THE TIMES

We were in Birmingham, the Cyril Stapleton Band doing a trade show. I think it was the Ideal Home exhibition.

There were about 8 of us sharing a room. It was a massive, cold, stark room so we decided to decorate.

Paul Brody, the drummer, and I were driving down the road late at night after a jar or two when we saw the ideal thing. It was a big road sign.

We got out of the car and put it on the roof and held onto it with one hand each out of the window.

It tried to take off a couple of times but I slowed down and we managed to get back to "Bleak House".

Our lead saxophone player was Jack Goddard. A really good solid sleeper. It was quite late and Jack had retired for the night in the dormitory.

So we tied the road sign to the bottom of his bed and in the morning he woke up and couldn't believe his eyes.

He thought he'd fallen asleep in the road: "NO LEFT TURN" was the first thing he saw.

Cyril Stapleton, 31 December 1914 – 25 February 1974.

Some Male Singers

❋ ❋❋❋❋❋❋❋❋❋❋❋❋❋❋❋❋❋❋

SACHA DISTEL

Google

Sacha Distel, 29 January 1933 – 22 July 2004.

I first met and worked with Sacha Distel, the jazz guitarist in 1967. He was a very good guitar player.

We made an album at IBC studios in Portland Place. The studios have long gone.

Many years later he sent me a copy of the album.

Over many years, Sacha and I appeared on lots of television shows: Val Doonican, Russell Harty, Parkinson and many more.

I was interviewed by Esther Rantzen on a special television show all about Sacha. Unfortunately, most of the comments were about his liaison with Brigitte Bardot.

He did have a ding dong with her at one time, but to him his guitar playing was what the programme should have been about.

He had a hit with the Bacharach and David song, "Raindrops Keep Falling On My Head". We featured it on the Parkinson show with my band.

Sacha was a good musician, he was very handsome, and that may have been a hindrance to his musical career. He died in 2004. It was good to know him.

❋ ❋❋❋❋❋❋❋❋❋❋❋❋❋❋❋❋

DICK HAYMES

I don't know why or how, but Dick Haymes and I became friends in about 1967. I think that I played the piano for him at American bases in the UK. He came to my Tudor cottage in Bray high street and we spent some time together.

Dick, who had been married to some of the world's most beautiful women, including Rita Hayworth, wanted a cigarette.

We had run out.

We went up Bray high street to a vending machine and bought ten Woodbines.

It seemed a trifle surreal that this person who had been married six times, to beautiful ladies, had been a phenomenally successful singer and actor, was buying ten Woodbines out of a machine in my high street.

Some day I will remember why we were together. At the moment I haven't a clue.

Some Male Singers

✻ ✻✻✻✻✻✻✻✻✻✻✻✻✻✻✻✻✻✻✻

JACK JONES

There are very few great crooners left in the world. One of them is Jack Jones. He is a friend of mine and I have known him for many years, mainly socially.

I only once played the piano for him. The phone rang and a charming lady with an Irish accent asked to speak to me. She told me that there was going to be a very important dinner the next night with a cabaret.

She said that two of the performers, who she had never heard of, had asked for me to accompany them. They were called Jack Jones and Sammy Cahn.

I told her I would be delighted to help them out and would be on a plane the next morning to the venue, the K Club.

After my arrival and short rehearsal with both Sammy and Jack, we were seated for dinner.

I had been Sammy Cahn's pianist on his one-man show so I knew his repertoire.

The evening was long. It dragged on and on and it was very late when there was an announcement that a band would now go on stage to perform.

Jack was furious. He and I went up to the organiser, an Irish gentleman who had had a lemonade or two. Jack said that if he didn't go on next then he wouldn't go on at all.

The gentleman said to the great Jack Jones, "Alright then, bugger off!"

We eventually did Jack's bit and Sammy and I did his bit.

Nobody was the slightest bit interested. Another memory, not so happy this time.

Some More Male Singers

❊ ❊❊❊❊❊❊❊❊❊❊❊❊❊❊❊❊❊❊❊

Wikipedia

JOHN LENNON

My late wife, Marion Montgomery, was the resident singer on the Parkinson television shows in the early 1970s.

One week the guests were John Lennon and his wife Yoko Ono.

As a tribute Marion sang "Love" – a John Lennon composition.

Some time later he sent Marion a card with just a hole in the centre, the size of a new penny.

All John had written was that the hole was there to see the sky through it.

A nice sentiment, I think.

I gave it to my daughter Abigail for posterity.

John Lennon,
9 October 1940 – 8 December 1980.

❊ ❊❊❊❊❊❊❊❊❊❊❊❊❊❊❊❊❊❊

ELVIS PRESLEY

I was in Las Vegas conducting my orchestra for Engelbert Humperdinck. We had a common green room to accommodate any visitors who might come to see the show.

Lots of "names" came to see the performance by Engelbert and one evening we heard that Elvis was in the audience.

He came backstage afterwards, and we were somewhat in awe of him and were very pleased to be with him.

He had his photograph taken with Engelbert and we were waiting for some words of wisdom from him.

He told us that he had on a new jacket and the material was real velvet.

That was it!

Not exactly the words of wisdom that we all expected, but the photo is elsewhere in this book.

❄ ❄❄❄❄❄❄❄❄❄❄❄❄❄❄❄❄❄❄

TOMMY STEELE

I got a call from Tommy Steele asking me to work with him on a television special. It was called *Quincy's Quest*.

The star of course was Tommy Steele as Quincy, the doll.

Some names of the cast were Mel Martin, Lance Percival, Matt Zimmerman, Roy Kinnear and loads more.

The story is about rejected dolls and this is the original synopsis:

It was the night before Christmas, and all toy store rejects are due to be tossed into the furnace. This includes Quincy, a most lifelike doll. In a last-ditch effort to save himself and his "unwanted" chums from incineration, Quincy goes on a long and perilous journey in search of the only one who can save them: Santa Claus.

A nice children's story, and I was the musical associate for the kudos and the fee that came with it.

We started to rehearse in September 1978 and finished the recording of the music in December of that year.

I was rather pleased with it when finished and the show went out a year later at Christmas.

with Lance Percival.

SESSION WORK -
AND WHO WAS IN CHARGE

❊ ❊❊❊❊❊❊❊❊❊❊❊❊❊❊❊❊❊❊

As a studio freelance session player I became a member of an elite group of special musicians.

We were people that could go into a studio at 10 am and be recording a piece of music which we had never seen before at 10.30 am.

The same group of musicians went from studio to studio recording with lots of different stars. We never knew until it was released, if we were part of a hit recording or a flop. I played the piano on most of the Tony Hatch–Jackie Trent hits. Usually featuring Petula Clarke.

We also did television series and film sessions.

One film session featured Sammy Davis Jr. The bass player standing right next to me was the great Frank Clark.

He leaned over and whispered in my ear "Laurie, look at his arse. I've got a dalmatian with a bigger arse than that!"

Another session bass player was Joe Mudele. He lived somewhere in South East London.

Look for the story on the next page about Charlie Katz...

❊ ❊❊❊❊❊❊❊❊❊❊❊❊❊❊❊❊❊❊

HARRY RABINOWITZ

Harry Rabinowitz was my mentor. Harry was the musical director of Rediffusion and then London Weekend Television.

We started at Wembley Studios with Rediffusion and then went to the South Bank as LWT.

The offices were just off the North Circular Road at Wembley. The most-used floor was at the top because that was where the bar was. Many glasses of champagne have been savoured at that establishment.

Harry was a genuine musical director. He played the piano, but not too well. He composed theme tunes, but not too well and he read a score as if it was a book. He read a score wonderfully.

I read a score horizontally, not very well, but Harry read a score vertically and could correct wrong notes easily by observation. That's why he was a musical director. He had been the MD of the BBC Concert Orchestra in the past, which involved conducting music of every kind, from classical to swinging standards. So, he was very qualified.

He didn't arrange as well as he might, so that's where I came in.

I arranged lots of music for his orchestra and I was his pianist. We got on very well.

A couple of stories about Harry:

We were asked to be the pit orchestra at the London Palladium for a Royal Command Performance.

The first half was perfect. At the interval Harry and I stayed in the pit and had a chat.

The band came back, probably from the pub, and we were all ready to start the second half.

The first act of the second half was a selection from a musical featuring Howard Keel, the singer. Harry must have heard some kind of cue to get ready. He thought it was the cue to start the music, and he did.

Wrong!

I had on a headset and the producer yelled in Harry's and my ear to stop! The curtain had begun to reveal the set and was hurriedly closed.

I presume that the Queen was not back in the royal box yet, hence the fiasco. Nothing was said about it. Just another goof.

※ ※※※※※※※※※※※※※※※※※※

I went to the Barbican to celebrate Harry's 90th birthday celebration. He was conducting the London Symphony Orchestra, one of his favourite bands which he had often used in the past. There had been many film scores which he had been asked to conduct.

After a while at the Barbican concert he decided that it was the interval time and started to leave the stage. The LSO members yelled at him to return as he still had one more piece to conduct before the interval. As usual, Harry carried the mistake off as if it was planned. Clever man.

Harry was of course conducting with the use of a baton. During the second half he hit his music stand with the baton which rebounded into the audience. Again, Harry was himself and was unconcerned, he carried on by just using just his hands.

Discography

Harry Rabinowitz, 26 March 1916 – 22 June 2016.

He was a very good friend. He remarried a lovely American lady called Mitzi Scott. They spent their winters in Portland, Oregon, and the summers at their home in France. I would have preferred it the other way round, but that was Harry.

He reached 100 years old. To celebrate, he was once again going to conduct the London Symphony Orchestra at the Barbican in London. I had bought two tickets.

One evening the phone rang and it was dear Harry. He asked me if I was able to do some arranging for him for the LSO concert. I told him that I would be honoured. I also told him that I had bought two tickets for the concert and jokingly asked if I would get my money back if he didn't last that long.

He sadly didn't.

Mitzi told me that he had an accident at home, was taken to hospital in Portland and peacefully died.

Good old Harry. A fine musician and a fine man.

CHARLIE KATZ

Each artist or orchestra had a music contractor. They got a fee for booking the musicians. Hours and hours on the phone. He was all-important as far as we the freelance musicians were concerned. If he liked the way that you behaved, dressed smartly and were punctual then, if you played well also you had a good chance of being on his list of employable musicians.

I fortunately was on several lists. One of the most important fixer was Charlie Katz. I had heard of him for years because he had a novelty sextet which had a regular BBC radio series.

He was very influential as a contractor/ fixer. He fixed the musicians for almost everybody and was a very strict disciplinarian.

So because I was presentable and played OK I was on his list.

One story I remember was of Joe Mudele, who lived south of the river and, horror of horrors, he was late for a studio session.

He apologised profusely to Charlie and explained that he was late because the Woolwich Ferry was late.

Charlie said "How dare you come to my session by boat!"

About 4 or 5 years ago Charlie's son rang me to ask if I would record a "Happy Birthday" piece for Nita, Charlie's wife, who was about to turn 100. (A private performance and so not subject to Warner/Chappell's license fee.)

Charlie had died many years before. I was delighted to be asked as I had been friends with Charlie for so long.

ALEC FIRMAN

The main musician contractor for London Weekend Television was a lovely man called Alec Firman.

He was definitely pro the musicians. He had a wonderful way of saying that we were entering an overtime period by pulling down on an imaginary bell. That silent "ding" meant extra money was being earned.

There was a very large orchestra booked for recording the music for "Fire And Ice", a skating programme. The session was coming to and end and any overtime would have been extremely costly.

But, just in time, it was completed to the relief of the managers in the studio recording booth.

But the musical director (it wasn't me!) asked the orchestra to re-do a short section which everyone was happy with, except him.

The managers were horrified as the clock ticked over to extra time and shouted "NO! NO! NO!"

The musical director didn't hear them and the resulting few minutes of recording cost the company thousands of pounds. Good for the musicians, not good for the budget.

PETER KNIGHT

Peter Knight was a wonderful, eccentric conductor and arranger. He was in great demand as a television special arranger. I knew him well because I was the pianist on a lot of his projects.

He had perfect pitch.

Apparently, when he was working on his musical arranging, he had to unplug his fridge because it clashed with his perfect pitch – it sounded a note which disturbed him. Foreign sound doesn't bother me, in fact I often write with the television on, for company.

Back to Peter.

He was born in Exmouth, Devon, and retained his wonderful accent throughout his life. I didn't realise, until I researched him, that he was born in 1917, so he was quite mature when I worked with him.

I wrote a television special called "The Dancing Princesses". I composed all the music on piano.

I asked Peter to arrange it for a full orchestra and he did his usual splendid job.

He arranged for many "pop" stars, amongst them were Scott Walker, The Carpenters and George Harrison.

He was the arranger and musical director of the very popular *Morecambe and Wise* television show.

A great arranger, a very nice person, sadly missed.

STUDIOS

❊ ❊❊❊❊❊❊❊❊❊❊❊❊❊❊❊❊❊❊❊❊

My first recording was with my good and oldest friend the singer Jackie Allan. I was 15 years old. We went to Manchester and recorded on an acetate.

The song was "With The Parting Of The Waves". I still have the acetate – it should be on the Antiques Road Show!

But the first proper commercial studio session I was involved with was *Juke Box Jazz*.

It was with the band I was resident with – Joe Daniels and His Hotshots. It was a well-known band of those days – the late 1950s. We played happy mainstream music. A Dixieland line-up of trumpet, clarinet and trombone with the rhythm section of piano, bass and drums. We recorded it at the famous Abbey Road EMI studios, long before a Beatle had been heard of. The record was played on juke boxes all over the country. The disappointing thing for me about it is the fact that the piano is nowhere to be heard! Ah well!

Then on to Cyril Stapleton. He was extremely well known because he had a regular radio series. He didn't have a band, he had an orchestra. We made quite a few albums. One featured me as soloist playing "Legend". I never had a copy and I can't find one so if you hear of one please let me know.

The musicians were engaged by a contractor and Cyril's contractor was called Charlie Katz. He was also a prolific band leader and had a very popular radio series with the Charlie Katz Novelty Sextet. I remember listening to them when I was a kid. We sometimes didn't know who the artist was because we did "backing track". This was so the artist could spend hours putting on his or her voice until it was acceptable. One of the lady singers I played for on lots of sessions was Petula Clarke.

My freelance studio life was in full swing. I recorded with lots of well known people

– Susan Maughan, Kiri Te Kanawa, Gilbert O'Sullivan, Cleo Laine and lots of other stars. I was the regular pianist on recordings for Stephen Sondheim. I wrote the music for a West End show called *Instant Marriage*. The book and lyrics were written by the late Bob Grant.

Retrocultural

Bob Grant, 14 April 1932 – 8 November 2003.

You would remember him as Jack in *On The Buses*. We were both in Lionel Bart's show called *Blitz* at the Adelphi theatre. Bob asked me to write the music to his lyrics and we then recorded them as a demo to plug for a possible producer.

On the last night of *Blitz* the impresario of the show, Donald Albery, came in to thank everyone and by chance we were playing our recording. Well he took it away and a week later told us that he and Brian Rix would like to produce it. It starred Joan Sims and lots of good old timers. We made a cast recording of it and it ran for a year at the Piccadilly theatre in London. Being a single bloke aged 24 it was rather nice to ask a girl if she would like to see my musical, a great chat-up line.

One of the memorable recordings I was on was with the jazz violinist Stephane Grappelli and the classical violinst Yehudi Menuhin. It was arranged and conducted by Nelson Riddle. Although Stephane and Yehudi played the same instrument they were utterly different in delivery. Stephane was "loose". He had a marvellous technique and great inventiveness in his jazz playing. He was a true jazz musician.

Yehudi as we all know was a fantastic classical violinist. But he only played the written notes. For this album he was asked to play ad lib jazz. That was a problem. He was helped by Max Harris writing out his now not-so ad lib jazz. It was all written down for him. He made a valiant attempt and the records were very successful.

I was the pianist for Judy Garland and Liza Minnelli for a series of concerts at the London Palladium. I spent 6 weeks with them, rehearsing and enjoying ourselves. I would turn up at Judy's house mid-morning and we would run through the songs until we had had enough and then go out to play. We often went to Danny La Rue's club.

The concerts were electric. There were a couple of numbers where Judy sat beside me on the piano stool. I became famous by association! Happy memories. There was an album made called *Judy And Liza At The Palladium*.

My late wife, Marion Montgomery, and I made lots of albums together. Marion always performed songs whose lyrics told a story and meant something to her. She was really a storyteller and didn't want to be called a jazz singer. Her last recording was made a few months before she left us. She sang songs that were really messages to her family. This one I believe was a message to our daughter Abigail: Hankies at the ready! *"How Deep Is The Ocean"*. I was part of the Gordon Mills organisation. He managed only three singers, but what a trio!

Engelbert Humperdinck, Tom Jones and Gilbert O'Sullivan. I was with Engelbert for five years. In that time I arranged several albums for him. When we were home from our travels I was asked to record with Gilbert O'Sullivan. He composed wonderful unusual songs. He very kindly sent me a few gold discs which are proudly hung in the place everyone hangs their discs – in the loo! One of the biggest hits I helped him with is *"Get Down"*.

Getty

Ronnie Corbett, 4 December 1930 – 31 March 2016.

I first saw Joe Williams in Birdland, New York when I was 18 years old. He was the singer with my favourite band The Count Basie Orchestra. It is amazing to me that later in life we became very good friends and I played the piano for him on many occasions. One of the great arrangers was Robert Farnon. I played piano on several Farnon projects and to my delight one of the albums was with Joe Williams called "Here's To Life". Incidentally in the recording box was George Shearing. Quite nerve wracking!

Kenny Lynch and I were mates for donkey's years. We did cabaret dates and played golf together. He was a one off! We made an album some time ago called *After Dark*. Kenny was in my opinion one of the best jazz-orientated singers in the business.

There's more detail about all this further on…

POLITICS

✳ ✳✳✳✳✳✳✳✳✳✳✳✳✳✳✳✳✳✳✳

THERESA MAY

Someone asked Theresa May and me, how we knew each other. We looked at each other and realised that we didn't know, because we had known each other for such a long time.

I suppose that we met when Theresa was canvassing and rang my doorbell to ask me to vote for her. She is my local Member of Parliament. I invited her into my house.

On the mantelpiece was a photograph of my friend John Prescott, the labour politician, and me. I told her that he was a very good friend, but that we never discussed politics, which is very true.

Another meeting was when we were together at my house, doing a radio interview for BBC Radio Berkshire.

We bump into each other at local stores and we go to the same butcher.

Only once was I at a meeting which she chaired as the local MP although she was at the time the Prime Minister. We were given instructions to say our names and what we did. I didn't know what to say about myself. A piano player? A musical director? An arranger? A friend of celebrities?

I was about the 12th to say who I was, and what I did. It came to my turn and before I could say anything she said "Hello Laurie." Relief, and bemusement by most of the others.

We see a lot of each other at Christmas parties and I get on well with Theresa's husband Phillip. She is still our local MP but has given up the role of Prime Minister.

I like her and Phillip a lot, long may it be so.

✳✳✳✳✳✳✳✳✳✳✳✳✳✳✳✳✳✳

CECIL PARKINSON

Cecil Parkinson, 1 September 1931 – 22 January 2016.

I first met Cecil Parkinson at our holiday home in the Bahamas at Treasure Cay.

We became quite friendly and at the time he was Mrs Thatcher's second-in- command and expected to be prime minister in due course. We arranged to have a game of golf. He turned up quite late and he didn't have the equipment for the golf game and asked me to lend him some balls. I said you are a future prime minister, you turned up late and have no balls.

I can't remember much about the game but he was a nice chap and I enjoyed his company.

✻ ✻✻✻✻✻✻✻✻✻✻✻✻✻✻✻✻✻✻✻

LORD JOHN PRESCOTT AND LADY PAULINE

John is a jazz fan. He was a fan of my late wife Marion Montgomery. That's how I know him. He lives in Hull and he would often turn up at concerts where we were appearing. He is the same age as me.

As mentioned, when we were both 18 we worked on the same cruise ship, the RMS *Carinthia*. We never met at that time, mainly because he was a waiter and lived below decks, and I was a piano player and lived at the posher end.

After the *Carinthia* John became a shop steward. He went to a university and eventually became a member of parliament. Because of his strong union connections he became the deputy prime minister under Tony Blair.

I'm still a piano player!

Through John, we became friendly with Betty Boothroyd and went to her home in the Commons for a knees up now and again.

While he was deputy Prime Minister, he was given the use of Dorney Wood House, and every New Year's Eve for ten years my wife and I were John and Pauline's guests. We had a great time, playing charades and having a dance after eating a fantastic dinner.

I had a phone call one day from John requesting my presence with him at Henley Regatta. He was doing a television show on Class and wanted to talk to the boater-wearing Hooray Henrys there. I suppose I was there to help him out of the river if he got pushed in. Fortunately he stayed dry.

My football team are Oldham Athletic. They were playing Hull and I had arranged tickets and parking by the secretary of the club, Alan Hardy. Then I thought that maybe John would like to go. He said he would and I arranged a ticket for him. I went to his house in Hull and we were driven to the ground in his rather famous Jaguar by his driver and security chap.

When we got to the car park the driver put his window down and said that he had Mr Prescott in the car and parking was arranged. The car park attendant said that no arrangements had been made for parking for Mr Prescott. I told the driver to say that he had Laurie Holloway in the car. The attendant said "come right in".

I don't think John was amused!

We are still in touch, mainly by telephone. Pauline is the one who I talk to most of all to find out how they are.

They are a great couple and it has been a pleasure to know them.

With the Prescotts at Dorney House.

Instant Marriage

❊ ❊❊❊❊❊❊❊❊❊❊❊❊❊❊❊❊❊❊❊

As you've read, in 1962 I was the pianist in Lionel Bart's Blitz! at the Adelphi Theatre on the Strand in London.

The male lead was Bob Grant, later known as Jack in On The Buses.

Bob and I hit it off and became good friends. He told me that he had written a book and lyrics of a farce called "Don't Ask Me Ask Dad". He needed the music written to a load of lyrics.

I was his man. I composed all the music and he liked what I had written.

We then made a demonstration tape in Denmark Street, the well-known Tin Pan Alley and finished up with a pretty decent recording of all of the songs.

Blitz! was about to finish its run. The producer of *Blitz!* was Donald Albery. He came to the theatre to thank everyone and to say his goodbyes.

At that particular time, I was with Bob Grant, in his dressing room, playing our tape of our potential musical farce.

Mr Albery was impressed. He asked if he could take a copy of it and listen to it elsewhere.

Within a week he got back in touch and told us that he and Brian Rix would like to produce it. Wow!

I was over the moon.

The title was changed to *Instant Marriage* and the cast included Joan Sims, Bob Grant, Wallas Eaton, Harold Goodwin, Paul Whitsun-Jones, Tony Holland, Stephanie Voss and Don McCorkindale.

After try outs at various theatres it was produced by Donald Albery and Brian Rix, the king of farce, at the Piccadilly Theatre in London's West End. The conductor was Gareth Davies. There were 366 performances.

The unlikely story is about four Yorkshire folk who come down to London on a day-trip and get into some ridiculous situations.

It's a genuine farce and resembles a "Carry On" situation with my music. The pianist in the pit was Martin Goldstein. He occasionally wanted a night off, so I was his deputy, playing my own songs. Great.

There was a weekly income which gradually dwindled because the box office takings dwindled. I was 26 and single, I didn't care.

I got quite friendly with the star, Joan Sims. Enough said.

Bob Grant, my co-writer, was a lovely man. For some dark reason he committed suicide.

A great talent, a great waste.

A West End musical and it's his first attempt

TUESDAY was a special "fingers crossed" evening for 26-year-old Greenwich pianist Laurie Holloway. For that was the night his first attempt at a musical was set before the jaded eyes of Fleet-street's critics.

And just for the night, Laurie himself was playing the piano in the pit at the Piccadilly Theatre for the 18 numbers in the new musical farce Instant Marriage.

Laurie, who lives in Tuskar-street, was playing the piano for the successful Bart musical Blitz! when he started working on Instant Marriage a year ago. Bob Grant, who had a leading part in Blitz! had an idea for a two-man review and asked Laurie to write some music. He did, but the plan was soon shelved in favour of a full-length musical.

When Blitz! ended, impresario Donald Arbury went backstage to chat with Grant, heard a tape of some of Instant Marriage, borrowed it—and came back five days later and said he wanted to put the show on.

S-trippers

"We had two weeks at Kilburn to start off but the place was like Carnegie Hall and Instant Marriage needs a more intimate atmosphere," Laurie told me. "It's very modern. Not West Side Story-modern but happy family-modern." The story concerns a Yorkshire family of trippers who come to London for the first time and get in-

Laurie Holloway

to endless troubles. An unmarried sister goes to a marriage bureau which, unfortunately, is in the same building as a strip club. Inevitably, she gets involved with the strippers. Stars include Joan Sims, Stephanie Voss, Bob Grant, Wallas Eaton, Paul Whitsun-Jones and Harold Goodwin.

Rock

Straight from school in Oldham, Lancs, Laurie joined summer season bands as a pianist. He played with Joe Daniels and then headed South for two years with Cyril Stapleton. He switched to accompany-

ing and worked with Anthony Newley, Susan Maughan, Marion Ryan, Bob Monkhouse and Cleo Laine before joining Blitz! Music in the new show varies from ballad and "bright" numbers to all-out ROCK. Said Laurie: "We've tried to get as much as we could into the show and we're hoping one number. Shake it about, is hit material." Book and lyrics for the show

were written by Bob Grant. With Donald Arbury in backing the venture is Whitehall Theatre "farce king" Brian Rix. "We'll give this a few weeks and then, if all goes well, start work on another musical," says Laurie.

Footnote: Laurie's parents are down from Lancashire to see the show—for the first time. Hope they stay clear of the strip clubs!

PICCADILLY THEATRE
DENMAN STREET, W.1
Telephone: GERrard 4506/7

Proprietors: PICCADILLY THEATRE LTD.

Managing Director and Licensee: DONALD ALBERY

DONALD ALBERY
(for Calabash Productions Ltd.)
and
BRIAN RIX
(for Brian Rix Enterprises Ltd.)

present

JOAN SIMS

PAUL WHITSUN-JONES   **BOB GRANT**

STEPHANIE VOSS   **REX GARNER**

HAROLD GOODWIN

in

INSTANT MARRIAGE
and
WALLAS EATON

A New Musical

Book and lyrics by   Music by
BOB GRANT   LAURIE HOLLOWAY

Directed by BOB GRANT

Musical Numbers staged by RAE LANDOR

Designed by DISLEY JONES

Orchestrations by ERIC ROGERS

Musical Director: Gareth Davies.

Lighting by Joe Davis

Some More Male Singers

❋ ❋❋❋❋❋❋❋❋❋❋❋❋❋❋❋❋❋

JOE WILLIAMS

Joe Williams was a good friend of mine. He was a great jazz singer.

I first heard him when I was a piano player on the Cunard Liner, RMS Carinthia. I was 18 years old. We used to dock in New York and immediately go up 52nd Street to the jazz club called Birdland. Joe was the singer with the swinging Count Basie band.

Great times.

Much later I became friendly with Joe and his wife Gill. She was very English, and a gorgeous lady. They were a handsome couple.

They lived in Las Vegas and as I worked there regularly with Engelbert we became good friends.

Much later I was asked to play the piano on an album arranged and conducted by Robert Farnon. I played on most of his projects.

I asked him who the artist was that we were going to accompany, and it was a great and pleasant surprise to learn that it was Joe Williams.

The album is called *Here's To Life.*

The only problem was that Joe was a foot tapping swinger and Robert was a very frilly arranger. Joe kept his eyes on me and when I nodded my head he knew that he was due to sing.

Not on every track, but some of them. The great George Shearing came to the session and I have a wonderful photo of the three of us.

With Joe Williams, 12 December 1918 – 29 March 1999, and George Shearing, 13 August 1919 – 14 February 2011.

Some More Male Singers

❋❋❋❋❋❋❋❋❋❋❋❋❋❋❋❋❋❋

SAMMY DAVIS JR

I was the pianist in the Harry Rabinowitz orchestra on the David Jacobs television series.

We had guest artists every week whom we accompanied. One week it was Sammy Davis Junior.

We accompanied this great talent and that was that …until Sammy, out of the blue, asked the audience for a song title because he was going to compose a song.

I knew nothing of it.

I think it was Donald Pleasance who suggested "Why Cry".

He turned to me and asked for a chord. I hadn't a clue what was going on, but I played a chord of "F".

He started to sing, and I played a sequence which he followed while he was making up some lyrics.

After eight bars he said to me that that was the verse, now for the chorus.

We then proceeded to compose a 32 bar tune that, I modestly say, was pretty good.

At the end of it the audience went berserk.

He told them that this young gentleman at the piano, me, and him, had never met and that I deserved their applause.

He said that he had only done that twice before. Once with Mel Tormé, and once with his musical director.

I was amazed that I had composed a song with the great Sammy Davis Jr.

He asked David Jacobs if he could have a copy of the song.

He was given a copy and so was I. The front of the TV Times was a photograph of him and me. It said, "A Moment of Magic".

I later met him again when we played golf together at Lake Tahoe, Nevada in the USA. We talked about the night that we wrote a song together.

He beat me at golf. I think I let him.

More happy memories.

At The Talk Of The Town – Sammy Davis Jr, 8 December 1925 – 16 May 1990.

When Things Go Wrong

✳ ✳✳✳✳✳✳✳✳✳✳✳✳✳✳✳✳✳✳✳

RAQUEL WELCH

I was the arranger for a television special featuring Bob Hope and Raquel Welch.

The band was conducted by Jack Parnell. I can't remember the arrangement I did for her, but she seemed pleased with the result.

As a means of showing her appreciation, in front of all my mates in the orchestra, she flung her beautiful arms round my neck and thanked me.

I was being hugged by the gorgeous Raquel Welch.

I could only say one thing …

I said "Raquel, you're standing on my foot."

I have said some stupid things in my time, but that was one of the most ridiculous.

✳ ✳✳✳✳✳✳✳✳✳✳✳✳✳✳✳✳✳✳

FRANK D'RONE

I was the leader of a small group at a new club owned by Annie Ross, the great jazz singer. It was in Covent garden and called "Annie's Room".

Wikipedia

Frank D'Rone, 26 April 1932 – 3 October 2013.

I was very young and a good pianist but not a good announcer.

We had vocalist guests and I was asked to do the announcing, but I chickened out and asked my good friend, my bass player Ken Baldock to help me out.

The current guest was an American singer called Frank D'Rone. He had in the audience a group of agents and representatives with a view to furthering his career.

My dear friend, Ken Baldock was ready to give him the big introduction. Instead of saying "Please welcome Mister Frank D'Rone," he said "Please welcome Mister Vic Damone"!

Oh dear!

Frank D'Rone and his entourage were furious.

After that, I did the announcing.

✳ ✳✳✳✳✳✳✳✳✳✳✳✳✳✳✳✳✳✳

When Things Go Wrong

❋ ❋❋❋❋❋❋❋❋❋❋❋❋❋❋❋❋❋❋

JACK DIEVAL AND AGNES SARKIS

There was a French jazz pianist called Jack Dieval, who was known as the Debussy of jazz because of his florid, lyrical style of playing.

He asked me to be musical director of a new album to be sung by his wife Agnes Sarkis.

Not only was I to be the musical director/arranger, but he also asked me to write the lyrics to four of his melodies.

Suddenly I was a lyricist!

I wrote all the arrangements, I wrote the required lyrics, and went to a recording studio in Paris to record his lovely wife, Agnes.

My backing singers were the Swingle Singers, a well-known vocal group.

All went well. I have the LP in my files. BUT … at a later date I heard that Jack had used all my tracks to make an album of his own as a piano feature.

I did get remunerated for the original album but got nothing for the one featuring Jack. I suppose that was a French way of doing things.

Jack died several years ago.

The lovely Agnes is still with us. Enough said!

❋ ❋❋❋❋❋❋❋❋❋❋❋❋❋❋❋❋❋❋

ROLF HARRIS

I started working with Rolf Harris in 1962.

We did a half hour radio programme on what I think it was then called the Light programme. Every week Rolf and my quartet got together and had a great time recording a show which went out later.

The producer was John Hooper followed by Bryant Marriott.

My quartet was basically Bobby Kevin on drums, Spike Heatley on bass, and Judd Proctor alternating with George Kish on guitar.

It was a happy time.

We used different studios. Aeolian Hall in Bond Street, the Piccadilly studio in Piccadilly and the BBC in Portland Place.

Rolf occasionally took time off to do other things and we accompanied at that time Lance Percival and Roger Whittaker.

We were asked by the BBC to do a pilot for a projected television series. I think it was Top of the Pops or something similar. We recorded in a BBC studio with an unknown group called The Rolling Stones.

I don't know what happened to the programme, but I do know what happened to the Rolling Stones

Rolf and I did a month at the Talk of the Town and an album came out of it. I have it.

We did lots of engagements together and Rolf was incredibly successful.

He had his fingers in lots of pies. Variety, animals, painting, hit records, everything.

Then he blew it!

He was accused of being a paedophile. He went to court and was found guilty and served part of a five year sentence. I knew nothing of his alleged behaviour. I was shocked and dismayed. He was in prison somewhere in the Midlands and I visited him there. I was utterly disappointed to have to buy him a cup of tea and a biscuit.

Eventually he had served his penalty and came home to his house down the road from me. I found it for him in the '70s.

I still see him and his lovely wife Alwen. We are still good friends. He served his time and regrets the past. He says that he is innocent. The jury thought differently.

He is my friend and that won't change.

❊ DRUGS AND MUSICIANS ❊

A few of my fellow musicians were sadly involved with drugs. Usually pot but sometimes harder stuff like heroin.

Two friends of mine were fairly heavily involved.

One was Phil.

He was a renowned percussionist and jazz drummer.

The story goes that he was playing percussion in the orchestra pit at a theatre in Manchester. The production was The King And I. Phil had a spot in the show to bang, very loudly, a large gong.

Unfortunately he had fallen asleep. He suddenly woke up and panicked.

He thought it was the cue for banging the gong.

It wasn't!

He banged the gong and the whole production stopped, wondering what was going on. Phil suddenly realised his enormous goof. He leaned over the orchestra pit rail and announced … "Dinner Is Served."

Unfortunately, because of his drug habit, I attended his funeral soon afterwards. My other friend on drugs was a brilliant guitar player, Dave.

We finished a David Frost television show and he went to one of his haunts to "turn on".

The stuff that he bought was a bad batch. He died almost immediately.

Great musicians. Sad stories.

Television

✳ ✳✳✳✳✳✳✳✳✳✳✳✳✳✳✳✳✳✳✳

My first ever television appearance was at the Finsbury Park Ballroom. I was 22 years old. I was in the Cyril Stapleton orchestra.

Cyril had a regular series called *The Melody Dances* and each week there was a featured soloist from the band.

My turn came and I played "Fascinating Rhythm". I was so nervous that I had to visit the loo before the start of the programme and be sick.

That was a good start to my television career.

The band was often used to accompany American visitors to the UK. I remember accompanying Connie Francis and one wonderful tour when the band accompanied Nat King Cole. Because Nat played the piano I was made redundant for his section of the show, but Cyril gave me a solo in the first half of the concert and because of Nat King Cole being there I was very nervous. but as I went on stage he told me to enjoy it, and I think I did. A wonderful memory which I related to his daughter Natalie Cole when I accompanied her many years later.

My dear friend Harry Rabinowitz was the musical director of London Weekend Television. I was his pianist and unofficial musical associate. It was a busy time in television because we did about three shows each week. David Frost was very much involved and we used to provide the music for *Frost On Friday, Frost On Saturday* and *Frost On Sunday*, all live shows, great experience and very exciting. The cast included The Two Ronnies, Frank Muir and Dennis Norden, and lots of big stars. I became friendly with Ronnie Barker and we recorded an album called *A Pint Of Old And Filthy*. Ronnie wrote the lyrics and I composed the music. I put a kind of theatre pit band together and did the arrangements for an album. Although it was somewhat corny music I had in my pit band great musicians – Don Lusher on trombone, Kenny Baker on trumpet and Ray Swinfield on woodwind, quite a band.

Pinterest

Sir David Frost OBE, 7 April 1939 –

David Frost's signature tune was written by George Martin of Beatles fame. I remember one of David's shows covered the moon landing live.

The guest singer on that show was the late Marion Montgomery who happened to be my wife. We had met in 1965 at a club in the west end of London called The Cool Elephant. The resident music was the John Dankworth Sextet and the Dudley Moore Trio. It was perhaps the happiest musical period of my life. Dudley was a great musician and we became good friends. His bass player was Peter McGurk and his drummer was Chris Karan. a swinging trio. John's band was Art Elefson on tenor sax, Johnny Marshal on trombone and of course John on alto sax. The bass player was Spike Heatley and the drummer was Allen Ganley and me on piano, quite a band.

All these television shows were done from the Associated Rediffusion studios at Wembley. When we moved studios to London's South Bank I was heavily involved in writing signature tunes for any new series. I composed the themes for *Russell Harty, Game For A Laugh, Watch Out, Beadle's About* and *Blind Date*. The producer was Alan Boyd.

I remember being called by Alan and asked to compose a signature tune for a new series called *Game For A Laugh*; there was an American version of it and he sent me a recording of the USA version.

The opening music was a complete song with lyrics so I composed something similar for our show. We were making a "pilot" which means that we were trying out the show before commiting it to the airwaves. On the day of the pilot I played my new song to Alan. It wasn't what he wanted so on the spot I wrote a catchy tune which he said was just right. It lasted for several series.

The four new presenters were Henry Kelly, Sarah Kennedy, Matthew Kelly and Jeremy Beadle, all fairly unknown at that time. The show was very successful and Jeremy Beadle was a star as a practical joker. Alan gave him his own series and asked me to compose the signature tune for that. I had a meeting with Jeremy and Alan and they told me it was going to be called *Watch Out, Beadle's About*. They wanted the music as soon as possible so I asked them to go for a cup of tea and come back in 10 minutes. In that time I composed the tune which lasted for the 14 years of the programmes.

On their return I played it on the piano and they liked it a lot. They said "Where are the lyrics?" I said go for another cup of tea! I then wrote these classical lyrics which will go down in history along with William Shakespeare's sonnets: *"Watch out ... Beadle's about, watch out ... Beadle's about. You'd better watch ... 'cos Beadle's about!"*

Around the same time Alan decided to make a series with Cilla Black called *Blind Date*. Again I was asked to compose the signature tune. That one lasted for 14 years. They were both Saturday night viewing so I was famous on Saturdays! I also wrote the signature tune for *Child's Play* for Michael Aspel. It was a busy time.

At the same time the BBC was doing lots of spectacular series with famous people. Val Doonican, Rolf Harris, The Two Ronnies, George Hamilton the 4th. The musical director for the BBC was Ronnie Hazlehurst. I played the piano on lots of them.

Jeremy Gibson-Beadle MBE, 12 April 1948 – 30 January 2008.

In 1970 Michael Parkinson was asked to do a series for the BBC. He asked me to be musical director for the series. His regular singer was my late wife Marion Montgomery. It was bad timing as I had just been contracted to go to the USA with Engelbert Humperdinck, so I missed writing the theme tune and it went to my friend Harry Stoneham. Harry did the show for the next ten years. He had a very nice small band and was a great asset to the show. When Michael's show returned after several years he asked me again to look after the music and this time I was more than pleased to be his musical director. We kept Harry Stoneham's signature tune because it was now the music totally associated with Michael.

When we started the series I had a five piece band. It is usual for programmes with music to eventually economise by reducing the size of the band. Michael did the opposite. We went from the five piece to a ten piece and then a wonderful sixteen piece swinging big band. Thank you, Sir Michael.

❊❊❊❊❊❊❊❊❊❊❊❊❊❊❊❊❊❊

STRICTLY COME DANCING

Because I was the only person with a big band on television I caught the eyes and ears of a new production. It was called *Strictly Come Dancing*. My agent asked me how I fancied being a dance band leader. I didn't fancy it!

I was invited to a meeting at the BBC Television Center and my agent persuaded me to go. The outcome was that I agreed to form a dance band and be the musical director of this rather strange new series. It had been a success in the '50s but now I was very dubious. Well it seems to have been a good idea! I did the first three series,

but it took all my time to write the arrangements for 14 dances each week and on top of that I was doing the *Parkinson* show. After three series I decided to call it a day and as we all know, it has gone from strength to strength. People ask me if I regret passing it up but I assure them that I don't. I now have time to spend doing other things like playing more golf.

When I was travelling with Engelbert in the USA we did lots of TV shows with the legends of the time. We did *The Dean Martin Show* and *The Pat Boone Show* and others, which due to our over-the-top enjoyment I can't remember.

Engelbert's shows were sold out every night of the five years I was with him.

We travelled all over the USA. We spent one month out of the year in Las Vegas, but the only gambling we did was playing bingo in between the two shows each night.

Tom Jones and Engelbert were with the same management and were kept apart for business reasons. The closest we got to each other was us being in Las Vegas and Tom being in Lake Tahoe, a few hundred miles up the road. We discovered that there was an English-style pub half way between us in Sacramento. Off we went after our last show at about midnight in a Lear jet and met Tom's entourage who had taken limousines to get to Sacramento.

We had a fierce darts match and imbibed a beer or two. Engelbert and Tom were very good darts players. Also very good snooker players, signs of their mis-spent youth.

After a couple of hours of fierce competition Tom's lot beat us on the last dart! A rare meeting of two good friends and their musicians. We enjoyed ourselves a liitle too much. Then back in the jet to the place we used to call "Lost Wages".

❊❊❊❊❊❊❊❊❊❊❊❊❊❊❊❊❊❊

The Nesbitts are Coming

YORKSHIRE TELEVISION

Member of the Trident Television Group

<u>YTV/ALL:</u>   <u>Thursdays from APRIL 17, 1980.   9.00pm.</u>

"THE NESBITTS ARE COMING"
****

A new six-part comedy serial, with original songs and music
produced by Yorkshire Television

***

· Devised and written by
DICK SHARPLES

With music composed by
LAURIE HOLLOWAY

***

Starring

MAGGIE JONES
CLIVE SWIFT
DEIRDRE COSTELLO
JOHN PRICE
CHRISTIAN RODSKA
as
The Nesbitts

and
KEN JONES
TONY MELODY
JOHN CLIVE
PATSY ROWLANDS
ARTHUR WHITE
as
"The Law"

Music Associate: Lyrics by
MARTIN GOLDSTEIN   DICK SHARPLES

Music arranged by LAURIE HOLLOWAY
***

Film Cameraman: Film Sound:
ALLAN PYRAH   DON ATKINSON

Film Editor: Film Dubbing Mixer:
ALLEN DEWHURST   ALAN BEDWARD

Designer: PETER CALDWELL

Produced and Directed by RONNIE BAXTER

/Contd...

Yorkshire Television Ltd.
The Television Centre
Leeds LS3 1JS

Telephone 0532 38283
Telex 557232

Television

❋❋❋❋❋❋❋❋❋❋❋❋❋❋❋❋❋❋❋

JAZZ 625

Humphrey Lyttelton, 23 May 1921 – 25 April 2008.

This was the new BBC2's flagship music experiment and the launch episode had none other than Duke Ellington's ensemble. To follow this up the next week, they decided to invite the top Britsh jazzers of the day on to the show and I was amongst them.

I was also privileged to be asked by John Dankworth to play the piano on a television special with two legends: the trumpeter Clark Terry and Bob Brookmeyer on valve trombone. Both American visitors.

On drums was my friend Allen Ganley and on bass was Rick Laird.

The *Jazz 625* programme was compered by Humphrey Lyttelton and was recorded with an audience at the Shepherds Bush BBC television studio.

We rehearsed in a pub and it was absolutely wonderful to play for these two great musicians. I was quite young, about 26 I think. What an experience.

❋❋❋❋❋❋❋❋❋❋❋❋❋❋❋❋❋❋❋

LES DAWSON

Les Dawson, 2 February 1931 – 10 June 1993.

I was the arranger for Les Dawson on Opportunity Knocks for the series in 1989.

Every week Les finished with a song which I had arranged for him. I didn't go to the recording in the studio as I had done my bit at home.

However, in 1990 I not only did the arranging, but I also played the piano on the show.

I got to know Les quite well. He was a better pianist than most people gave him credit for. It's not easy to play the wrong notes on purpose.

Apparently, he learned that talent when he was playing the piano in a brothel in Paris. When he played wrong notes the listeners laughed, so he developed that into his act.

So he said.

❋❋❋❋❋❋❋❋❋❋❋❋❋❋❋❋❋❋❋

Television

✳✳✳✳✳✳✳✳✳✳✳✳✳✳✳✳✳✳✳

OSCAR PETERSON

Discogs

Oscar Peterson CC CQ OOnt,
15 August 1925 – 23 December 2007.

On the Oscar Peterson television series I was asked to play the piano for a French flautist, the great Jean-Pierre Rampal.

I had previously recorded the *"Suite for Flute and Jazz Piano Trio"* with Elena Duran, a very talented Mexican flautist.

The suite is a composition by the French pianist Claude Bolling. M. Rampal had previously recorded it with M. Bolling.

Jean-Pierre was asked to play *Javanaise* from the same suite.

I was booked to accompany him, along with my friends Allan Walley on bass and Allen Ganley on drums.

Javanaise is a roast! It is in 5/4 and rather difficult.

But it was a success. At the end Oscar Peterson (no other) said he was glad he didn't have to play it!

I can't remember the scheduled 2nd piece that Jean-Pierre was going to play, and which I had rehearsed, but he decided to change his mind.

Instead we played a piece which I had never seen before. I was sight reading! It must have gone alright as it was accepted.

✳✳✳✳✳✳✳✳✳✳✳✳✳✳✳✳✳✳

CANNON AND BALL

There was a new double act called Cannon and Ball who were going to do their first television show. I was asked to be their first musical director.

It was good to see their progress and I remained friendly with them.

Sadly Bobby Ball died in late october 2020 but I like to think I'm still friends with Tommy Cannon.

✳✳✳✳✳✳✳✳✳✳✳✳✳✳✳✳✳✳

Television

✻✻✻✻✻✻✻✻✻✻✻✻✻✻✻✻✻✻✻

STRICTLY COME DANCING

I've already mentioned that the BBC had ideas to start a new television series called *Strictly Come Dancing*. That was in 2003. It was named after an old series which was called *Come Dancing*.

I was the only musical director with a television big band as I was already doing the weekly *Parkinson* programme.

They got in touch with my agent, Ann Zahl, and asked her if I would be interested. I told her that I was definitely not a dance band leader and that I was not interested in the least.

She said that I should give it a go and against my better judgement I agreed, and went to the first production meeting.

I settled for a band that was lighter on the blowing front but very heavy on the rhythm section numbers. This was to provide the engine room for Latin and Ballroom dancing.

The routine was this. The young producers would select the songs for each dance.

The song was sent to Graham Jarvis to reduce electronically to one and a half minutes of the most recognisable section. Graham then sent it to me as an email and I then arranged it for my band.

This could be somewhat confusing for the dancers as they were rehearsing to the original recorded singers, and on Saturday they were dancing to the same routine but to a different sound.

For example a Beatles song would be arranged for my dance band, a different sound altogether. It didn't seem to bother anyone as they were probably so nervous and focused that they just carried on regardless. The show was "live" which is great because you know when we start and when we finish. No re-takes!

I was arranging 14 dance titles per week and also writing the *Parkinson* play-ons.

I later got wise and asked my band pianist, Malcolm Edmonstone, and band saxophonist, Duncan Lamont Junior, to relieve me of several charts each week.

That was better, a little more time for family and golf.

The presenters were Bruce Forsyth and Tess Daly and the singers were the wonderful Tommy Blaize and Lance Ellington.

Bruce I had known for years but now we were together on a weekly basis. He was a pretty good pianist and we bonded immediately.

Tess and I never got to know each other, for some reason. One series she was replaced by Natasha Kaplinski, the news reader.

After 3 series of *Strictly* I was getting a bit jaded. I was still doing the *Parkinson* series. I really enjoyed doing both shows but I never had much time to see my growing grandsons.

So I resigned from *Strictly* and stayed with *Parkinson*.

Would I still be doing *Strictly* if I had chosen the other way? I doubt it. Enough was enough.

Even Bruce had had enough and left. I believe that he and I are the only 2 people to leave voluntarily.

Little did I know that *Parkinson* was about to end. So I went from being a very busy musical director/arranger/ pianist, to being very much unemployed.

I was now very available for my grandsons and golf matches...

Some Photos
From My Album

With Ian McShane.

With Michael Parkinson, and Paul McCartney.

With Buddy Greco.

With Stephane Grappelli..

With Cab Calloway.

With Gerri Mulligan.

With Barry Mason.

With Alfie Boe.

Golf - and Other Triumphs and Failures

❄❄❄❄❄❄❄❄❄❄❄❄❄❄❄❄❄❄❄

I started to play golf too late to be really good at the game. The bass player Joe Mudele gave me a book by Ben Hogan and a seven iron and told me to read it and practice.

He and I became members of a nine- hole course called Shortlands. I loved it. I've never had a hole in one but came close to it at Shortlands.

There was a seasoned pro, Reg, who made my first set of wooden clubs. Not many pros could do that today.

Most showbusiness celebrities play golf, because they usually have their shows in the evenings and have the afternoon free. I got Engelbert interested in golf and got my local pro, Jack Hawkins to give him lessons. He built a sand trap in his garden and became most proficient. When he was about my standard we had a $100 game to decide who was the better player. On one hole my ball landed in a stream against a rattle snake. He won!

We once played Pat Boone and his musical director in Las Vegas. They were so slow that we left them and carried on as a twosome. Not ethical but we were a bit unethical at the time.

I have made many showbiz friends through playing golf. Two of the best players were Val Doonican and Jimmy Tarbuck. I played piano on Val's television series, and each year I went to Portugal to play golf in the Jimmy Tarbuck classic.

My neighbour and good friend Sir Michael Parkinson and I are members of our local course, Temple Golf Club. We once played with Tony Jacklin and he had a putt of about 18 inches. I told him to take it away as he wouldn't miss it. He told me that professionals were never given putts on the tour, so he declined my offer and of course sank it.

My late friend Kenny Lynch and I spent many happy hours playing Temple. We had similar swings and similar handicaps.

My lady golfing partner was Patricia. Boy was she aggressive? We often played in Temple

Kenny Lynch pointing to my name in gold.

Peter Alliss ran lots of tournaments to which I was invited as a celebrity.

tournaments and won one, gold paint on a board for ever. Patricia has gone to that great fairway in the sky. I hope that she is still knocking it down the middle.

My current golfing partner is Chris Osborne. He is a mature 71 and plays off 4. Fantastic.

My handicap has been 11 but is now soaring upwards, probably due to my age and lack of fitness. I still enjoy it though. Good fresh air and camaraderie.

Golf has been important in my life, still is, even though I'm useless now. I have played and met many "names" through golf: Chi Chi Rodriguez, Jack Nicklaus, Pat Boone, Sir Jackie Stewart, Jerry Lewis, Lee Trevino.

My drummer and I were watching television in Las Vegas when Trevino missed a 4-foot putt and lost the tournament by one shot. That night he came to the show and of course we cheekily asked him how he could have missed that putt. He was less bothered than we were because he was still very rich and there was another week for him to play and win.

Frankie Vaughan had an annual tournament in which I played many times. Peter Alliss likewise. He and his wife Jackie ran lots of tournaments to which I was invited as a celebrity. I would stand on the first tee and my fellow playing team would want to know what I did. Celebrity?

Golf. The great leveller.

With Nick and Michael Parkinson and Kenny Lynch.

S.S.S. 69 White Tees / 67 Yellow Tees — Please Tick which Tees ☐ played off

Date... JULY 11TH 1976
Handicap... 17
Strokes rec'd... 17

PLAYER L. HOLLOWAY (IN BLOCK LETTERS)

COMPETITION VANSITTART NEALE

Marker's Score	Hole	White Tees	Yellow Tees	Par	Player's Score	Stroke Index	Win+ Half O Lose- or Points	Marker's Score	Hole	White Tees	Yellow Tees	Par	Player's Score	Stroke Index	Win+ Half O Lose- or Points
	1	383	329	4	4	9			10	246	199	3	4	10	
	2	428	385	4	4	5			11	416	392	4	5	2	
	3	350	301	4	5	13			12	507	484	5	6	6	
	4	484	483	5	4	1			13	139	122	3	3	18	
	5	143	139	3	4	17			14	358	343	4	4	12	
	6	392	315	4	5	15			15	392	317	4	4	4	
	7	326	303	4	4	7			16	232	223	3	4	14	
	8	229	215	3	3	11			17	414	394	4	4	8	
	9	500	416	5	6	3			18	261	256	4	3	16	
	OUT	3235	2886	36	39				IN	2965	2730	34	37		
									OUT	3235	2886	36	39		
									TOTAL	6200	5616	70	76		

NOTE: Par at the 9th Hole from the Forward Tee is 4.

Marker's Signature...
Player's Signature...
CHECK YOUR SCORES

| HANDICAP | 17 |
| NET SCORE | 59 |

PLEASE:— Replace Divots, repair Pitch Marks, and let Faster Matches through.

G2001

My best score card ever!

TERRY WOGAN

I really don't know where to start. Perhaps I should start when we became neighbours. Terry and Helen moved into the same road as me, about 1978. They lived four houses away from me.

My daughter Karon Julie became the babysitter for their children.

Google

Sir Terry Wogan KBE DL,
3 August 1938 – 31 January 2016.

Terry joined my golf club and we regularly had a not so friendly match. In the clubhouse there are the so-called "gold" boards.

If you win a competition you get your name in gold paint on the relevant board.

Terry's name is on one board. He and I played in a competition and he came second.

The board that was dedicated to that competition had the names of first and second written on it, so Terry got his name for eternity on a board in the club house.

Unfortunately, Terry's name is about six inches off the ground, so he said that you had to get on your knees to read it.

I had a radio in my kitchen and I often listened to Terry's programme.

I coined the phrase "Terry Wogan's Investment Trust" or "TWIT" - I often wonder if that was the beginning of "TOGS" or Terry's Old Geezers which became his property.

Terry and Helen moved from Bray to Taplow. They lived in a big house with a view over Berkshire to Windsor Castle. Rather fitting, because the Queen invested Terry with a knighthood. Well deserved.

We often went to dinner at their house and generally became a clique.

Terry had a television talk show on three days each week, and I was his musical director whenever there was a musical guest.

Marion and Helen, along with other lady friends, lunched regularly. He and I met less often after my wife Marion had died.

Terry died in January 2016. The nation mourned the loss of a dear friend.

My wife Maryann and I were invited to Terry's memorial service at Westminster Abbey. Lots of friends were there to pay respects to a lovely man and a dear friend.

BRUCE FORSYTH

Dear Bruce Forsyth had made a new album in the USA. He was very pleased with it and wanted me to listen to it, so he asked me to go to his house at Wentworth estate on Wentworth golf course.

We spent a lovely afternoon listening and talking, and after a while Bruce suggested that we should play a few holes of golf.

So off we went in his private buggy, not to the first hole but to the second. If we had gone to the first he or I would have had to pay!

Crafty old devil!

JIMMY TARBUCK

Jimmy Tarbuck promoted, for charity, a golf week in Portugal. I used to go every year. It is a marvellous diversion from working in the recording studios.

There were lots of "names" there: Henry Cooper, Bobby Moore, Kenny Lynch, Denis King, Cliff Thorburn, Michael Parkinson, Laurie MacMenemy, Tony Dali, Susan Maughan, Frankie Vaughan, Robert Powell, Tim Brooke-Taylor, Dennis Waterman, and lots of other stars. We generally played golf with paying punters and then ate and drank.

My main contribution to the week was playing piano for the cabaret on Friday evening.

One year I took my young attractive niece who was going through a difficult divorce. Of course no one believed it was my brother's daughter and quietly suggested that I was cheating on my wife Marion. Later in the week I was vindicated as she met and later married one of the golfers, Eddie Hubery.

A memorable round of golf for me was a three ball. Me with Michael Parkinson and Bobby Moore the legendary footballer. It was not long before he died. Mrs Moore was with us and it will always be a happy memory of time spent with him.

One day I was chatting to the football manager, Laurie MacMenemy, and a passing wit said "Look there, two articulated Lauries."

Ha Ha.

❋❋❋❋❋❋❋❋❋❋❋❋❋❋❋❋❋❋

MICHAEL BARRATT

Michael Barratt is one of my best friends. We lunch together every couple of weeks.

We love to gossip and have the odd libation. I have known Michael for about fifty years.

I remember him being in my sitting room and telling me that he was going to front a new television programme called Nationwide. It ran for years.

He was with Robin Day on Panorama and also on 24 Hours. He was the chairman of the BBC radio programme Gardeners' Question Time.

He is possibly one of the worst golfers I have ever played with, and surprisingly he wrote a golf book with Tony Jacklin, the famous and successful golfer.

Whenever we hold a party at my house, usually musical, he gets the ball rolling with his favourite song "Roll A Silver Dollar". His singing is marginally better than his golf.

He had his own production company and I wrote a lot of his signature tunes. He is the father of nine chilren, two wives delivering six and three.

Marvellous.

He is slightly older than me and I love him to bits.

With Michael Parkinson and Michael Barratt.

❋❋❋❋❋❋❋❋❋❋❋❋❋❋❋❋❋❋

FOOTBALL - THE BOYS OF '66

England won the World Cup in 1966, I was a session piano player at the time.

I had a friend called Don Black, a very successful lyricist, whose brother Michael Black was an agent. I asked Michael if he could get tickets for the England matches at Wembley. He called me and said that I was in luck as he had got a ticket for every England match at Wembley.

I was ecstatic. What I didn't know was that my ticket was in the middle of a Mexican block.

I soon learned to shout "Ole!" but when the Mexican team was eliminated, I was able to shout "Come on England!" The England team went from strength to strength and reached the final of the World Cup.

I had a session booked by Charlie Katz for the very same afternoon. Charlie was a stickler for correctness and with great trepidation I asked to be released so that I could go to the final. Good old Charlie, he let me off and booked somebody else to play the piano. As you must know, England won, and we all went berserk.

Fast forward to much later – 1986. A television programme had been made about the route of the England team to the final. It was fronted by my friend Mr Parkinson, now Sir Michael.

I composed the music and my friend Ray Swinfield played woodwind on it.

I composed anti-action music. Almost gentle.

I think it was the first time that such music had been put on an action documentary. I like to think so anyway.

The boys of '66, what a wonderful team.

Ray Swinfield, 14 Dec 1939 – 4 Oct 2019.

London Jazz News

GREYHOUNDS

Ted Rogers had a very successful television show called *3.2.1*. I was the musical director for the six years it ran.

Each week I would travel to Leeds the night before the show, and go with the producer, Mike Goddard, to the Leeds dog track. He owned a dog which he had called Dusty Bin.

The trainer told me that he had a dog for sale, and I told him that I wasn't interested in owning a greyhound. Several glasses of Champagne later, I bought a greyhound called Final Hope. The Champagne had made me somewhat reckless.

I was travelling weekly up to Leeds when the show was running, for the next six years. I used my band from London. We were incorrigible. We got fish and chips from a chippy which was run by two fat ladies. We drank for England, but behaved ourselves at showtime.

One day, the musical director of the Yorkshire Television station realised that there was an extremely competent musical director based in Leeds. I was relieved of my position. The company saved quite a bit of money because there were no travelling costs and no accommodation charges for me.

My problem was that I owned a greyhound.

The solution was that I took my dog to Berkshire and found a local trainer who ran it at Slough Dog track.

The new trainer kept me informed of Final Hope's welbeing. He told me that Final Hope was going to win in a certain race, but don't ask him how he knew.

I didn't ask him, but I told my good friend J J Warr, and he said that there was a certain bookmaker and he would love to take his money.

We went to the track, Final Hope romped home, J J Warr had his revenge and I was the proud owner of a winning greyhound.

I won about £15.

Bliss.

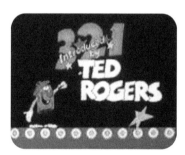

Ted Rogers, 20 July 1933 – 2 May 2001.

SHOOTING

I shoot. Since I was a kid I have had a pellet gun, mainly for shooting at a paper target.

When I was in Weymouth doing a season with Cyril Stapleton I became friendly with a local farmer, Bill Munts. He showed me how he enjoyed shooting and went with me to Dorchester to buy my first double- barrelled shotgun.

I gave it to my grandson Freddie a few years back.

I joined a shooting club and learned how to shoot properly. We were shooting at clays which were fired from high towers.

Because of a friendship with Edward and Patricia Cook, (she was a singer), I was invited to their very social shooting weekends. They were American citizens. Edward was extremely wealthy from various business ventures, one being the first grain exporter from the USA to Russia. They had bought the Manor house at Great Rissington and enjoyed befriending royalty and aristocracy.

They had a shoot to which I was regularly invited. I shot alongside Andrew Parker Bowles. Winston Churchill junior and Prince Michael of Kent and other guests.

The routine was thus:

Arrive on Friday for tea. The butler took our luggage to our rooms and unpacked for us.

Drinks at 7pm, black tie dinner afterwards until about 10pm.

The ladies were then taken out of the dining room by Patricia and we men passed the port and some smoked good cigars and then to bed.

Saturday, a help yourself breakfast of everything you desired. The whole lot. After a short break we drew straws for pegs.* I always hoped for an outside of 8 pegs to start.

It was early, I was slightly suffering from an excess of port and I wasn't a terribly good shooter.

We were ushered into transport to the first of maybe 6 different locations for shooting pheasant. The pheasant were driven by the game- keeper and his assistants.

The assistants became known to me because after each drive we would have a short break for a snack, which was usually champagne and sausage rolls. I started to feel better.

As I said, I am not in the same league as some of the shooters. They would be successful business people and usually "upper class". They had been born with a double barrel shotgun in their cot.

The best shooter I have seen was Hugh van Cutsem, a friend of Prince Charles. If I missed a bird he would turn around and get it without fail.

Someone else was using a gun that once belonged to *the* Winston Churchill. I asked his loader how the famous gun was doing.

The loader said that it wasn't doing him much good! He wasn't too good a shooter.

We went back to the manor for lunch. Usually very masculine fare. A hearty pie and loads of potatoes. More after lunch drinks.

Back to the shooting fields at about 2 pm.

We only had a couple of drives in the afternoon because of the shortness of the day and oncoming dusk.

The game-keeper told us the size of the bag and asked if we would like a brace to take home.

We then tipped him, the sum dependant on the size of the bag. Usually a pretty large bag and pretty large tip.

Back to the manor house. Shower and relaxation for a while.

Believe it or not, drinks at 7-ish. Black- tie dinner and then I would play the piano for a while.

> **Edward Cook,**
> **19 June 1922-8 March 2001**
>
> *For a pheasant or partridge driven shoot you will be placed at a stand known as a peg, usually marked by a number. The peg is a ground marker that you will stand at during the drive. Many shoots have different ways of moving guns from drive to drive, so make a note of what peg you will start from and which you will move to for each drive.*
>
> A. Hume *Shooting Etiquette*

I remember once I played an eight- minute Beatles Medley. Applause at the end and one person asked me if I could play something by the Beatles.

It takes all kinds!

Bed, breakfast and then to the local church.

We would leave late morning and recuperate ready for the next social shoot.

Most of my hosts have gone to the great pegs in the sky.

As a postscript I must tell you about my current invitations.

I do proper shooting - Eight of us meet at a pub for lunch. We each pay for the meal.

We then go to the shooting ground which is owned by two of the men. This is a rough shoot.

Walk, see an occasional pheasant, have a bang at it, probably miss it, count our bag at dusk, we might have six or seven birds, say our goodbyes and go home. Proper old fashioned shooting.

I do miss the champagne though!

Gordon Mills

❊❊❊❊❊❊❊❊❊❊❊❊❊❊❊❊❊❊

TOM JONES, ENGELBERT HUMPERDINCK & GILBERT O'SULLIVAN

I was asked by Gordon Mills to be the musical director for Engelbert Humperdinck. Let me tell you how it came about. Gordon Mills had been a harmonica player with a mouth-organ group called The Viscounts.

He was Welsh, and had a friend who said that he had heard a fantastic singer in a Welsh club. The singer was called Tom Woodward and Mr Woodward was looking for a manager. Gordon signed him.

The film *Tom Jones* was big news at the time and Gordon was very much a man who liked to be in charge, so he changed the name of Tom Woodward to Tom Jones.

Quite a successful move.

Gordon was co-composer of a song called *"It's Not Unusual"* with Les Reed. It was written for Sandie Shaw and Tom did the demo recording for her to listen to. She was impressed by Tom's version and told Gordon Mills to release that version.

Tom Jones was born.

At the time I was a successful session and television freelance piano player.

There was another singer called Gerry Dorsey who was reasonably successful. Doing the odd television spot, but struggling to be a star. I think he got in touch with Gordon Mills and asked if he would represent him.

Gerry was very handsome and had a good voice. Gordon signed him and changed Gerry's name to Engelbert Humperdinck.

The original Engelbert Humperdinck was a composer. His most famous composition was the opera *Hansel and Gretel*.

So Gerry became Engelbert.

It was 1967 and because of someone's illness Engelbert Humperdinck was asked to appear on Sunday Night at the London Palladium.

He sang an old country and western song. *"Please Release Me"*. It was a sensation.

This good looking chap with a really good voice was an overnight sensation. He suddenly was in great demand as the *"Please Release Me"* record was Number One in the charts.

He was doing a television series for ATV with the great Jack Parnell band. His arranger was my good friend Arthur Greenslade.

The weekly routine was to record the show, have a day off, then pick the titles for the next week. But this didn't happen. Arthur was not given the titles until late in the week.

He had to arrange several big band charts in such a short time that it got the better of him and he wasn't well, so Gordon asked me to take over.

I might look an easy touch but I laid down some conditions.

The show was done on Saturday. Sunday was a day of rest. But I insisted that on Monday morning I would meet with Gordon and go away with the titles for me to arrange for next Saturday. It seemed to work.

The charts were done and I stayed sane. End of series.

There was a young songwriter who was impressed by Gordon Mills and his Midas touch and asked Gordon to be his manager. His name was Ray O'Sullivan. Gordon was impressed by the tunes that Ray wrote, signed him on and changed his name to Gilbert O'Sullivan.

I have been a friend of Ray/Gilbert for 50 years. Gilbert has a small backing group but when he performs with a big orchestra, I get the phone call.

Once upon a time Gilbert wrote a song called *"Get Down"*. My rhythm section played the backing because Gilbert wasn't there. Gilbert says that is my claim to fame. It is a good story but I have done other things in my life.

Over many years I have recorded with Gilbert/Ray.

He always composes in a key which is a semitone down, or up, I can't remember. I therefore go home and transpose the chords to the right key and then do the arrangement. Not easy, but good experience.

I am still in touch with all three of the singers.

PEGGY LEE

I have arranged lots of tunes for Gilbert. He is a big fan of Peggy Lee.

He told me he had written a song as a duet for the two of them. Would I help him with it?

I spoke to Miss Lee and fixed a key over the phone. She has long been a favourite of mine so I was thrilled to be working with her.

Of interest is that Peggy Lee "discovered" my first wife, Marion Montgomery, and got her signed to Capitol Records in the USA, where she had a few hits.

With Engelbert and Ase O'Sullivan, Gilbert's wife.

*With Gilbert (Ray) on his birthday
(note the "R" on the cupcake).*

interview

LAURENCE
HOLLOWAY
WAS

↓

HERE

↑

*Almost famous again – the curse of the picture editor in the act of framing Engelbert and Elvis.
The hotel staff managed to get themselves in!*

Gordon Mills Tries Diplomacy

❋❋❋❋❋❋❋❋❋❋❋❋❋❋❋❋❋❋

GETAWAYS

Whenever we had any time off on the Humperdinck tours we were "shipped out" of the USA to some exotic, sunny, don't-drink-the-water spot. We had to get out of the States for Englebert's tax reasons. One of our getaway places was Venezuela.

After an exhausting few months on the road were all ready for fun and frolics in the sun, and a few tropical rum punches to pickle the germs. So off we went to Venezuela. We were all lined up to stay some way out of Caracas on the north coast.

On the plane, caviar and champers, poker, jokes and relaxation at last. We landed at the airport in wonderful spirits and went like a dream through immigration (they usually had been alerted to our arrival) and then into customs.

We never had anything to declare because there was no point in us collecting gifts when we still had months to go before we would be home.

Most of us had gone through the gate when we saw that Englebert's valet had been asked if he had anything to declare.

"No of course not," he answered, but they asked if he would mind if they had a look. Ah well, just a short delay before we could hit the beach. The customs man went through a few bags and all was OK.

Just one quick look in the hand baggage. Uproar! Englebert always carried a selection of pills for his throat and some antibiotics, all kept in a red leather case of small containers.

What were these interesting drugs, asked the man. The valet told him they were quite harmless tools of the trade for Mr Humperdinck. So the silly customs man immediately thought: pop group, pills – drugs!

We were all called back through the gate and asked to wait in a room. In this room we were watched over by three guards with very dangerous-looking pistols. We were not informed as to what was going to happen and were kept there for ages.

Gordon Mills, 15 May 1935 – 29 July 1986.

At last a chap came along and told us that we would now leave, so off we went out of a back door – straight into a Police van!

I am not by nature a coward, but this really had me scared. I thought the germs in the water were already starting to take effect and I hadn't drunk any yet! We had a fairly long drive and finished up in a really seedy area somewhere (I still have no idea where it was) and we were taken into prison.

Where was our lovely beach, our exotic rum punch, what on Earth was happening?

The inside of the jail was a perfect example of the ones you see in the movies. There was a very slow-moving ceiling fan, the faded yellow paint was peeling off the walls, nobody in charge spoke a word of English, and, wait for it, cockroaches!

I was terrified.

The debauched-looking Police took Englebert into another room and interrogated him, under one of those lamps you see in spy movies. They insisted that as he was a pop star and carrying a quantity of pills, then there must be some goings-on.

This next bit may be a bit hard to believe but it is perfectly true. I walked out!

Nobody seemed to be paying much attention to me so I did a few circuits of the room, peered out of the door and just walked out. Incredibly, a taxi came round the corner and I hailed it and thought the best thing I could do would be to go to the hotel. As soon as I got there (no I didn't go to the bar) I got on the phone to the British Ambassador in Caracus.

I explained what was happening to a chap there and he said that the Ambassador was at dinner but he would contact him and get things moving. Then I called the London office of Englebert's company and told them to get in touch with Gordon Mills.

Then I went to the Bar!

Well, things soon started to happen. A doctor was called to examine the drugs and he pronounced them harmless. (I don't know why they didn't do it at the airport.) Then the "convicts" were released and soon joined me at the bar. At last we had our exotic paradise, our sunny clime, our relaxation and fun. Nothing could spoil the next few days, we would escape from "the road" for a while.

Then came instructions from London: Catch the next flight out of the country. Gordon Mills had virtually made Britain break off diplomatic relations with Venezuela!

There was going to be an almighty fuss so we should get out of the way pronto. I downed the beautiful dregs of my Green Bombo, packed away my swimsuit and we all roared into the airport and onto a plane, chased by The Press.

That was one of our delightful getaway places crossed off the list.

Still, there were lots more and we made full use of them.

Engelbert and me in recent years.

Charity and Pastoral Work

✵✵✵✵✵✵✵✵✵✵✵✵✵✵✵✵✵✵✵✵

BRINSWORTH HOUSE AND TEDDY AND PEARL

There is a home for retired and dependant ex-theatricals. It is called Brinsworth House, in Twickenham, South London.

Every Monday they have a short performance by various people that are only too pleased to shed some sunshine into their lives.

It was until recently organised by a lovely ex-actress called Joy Francois. She asked if I would be interested in doing a short performance there. I have now been four times.

I have done the show with Kenny Lynch, Barry Mason, Tina May and one solo performance. Some of my old friends are "guests" there.

It is a charitable establishment paid for by the Artistes' Benevolent Society. The president is Laurie Mansfield. The famous married duo, Teddy Johnson and Pearl Carr were residents there.

In 1959 they came second in the Eurovision song contest with the song "Sing Little Birdie".

I thought it would bring back happy memories for them if I played it.

I did, but unfortunately time had taken its toll and they couldn't remember it.

The Advertiser, August 2, 2002   5

Stars roll up for Parky's day at the crease

GOOD TIMES: Laurie Holloway and Michael Parkinson enjoying one of the many celebrity cricket matches which have been an annual event in Bray for more than 25 years. Ref:72291/(1)/20

DOZENS of celebrities are expected among the crowds in Bray this Sunday as the village hosts Michael Parkinson's annual celebrity cricket match.

Well-known figures from the worlds of sport, stage and the small screen will be joined by top businessmen for the event at Maidenhead and Bray Cricket Club, in Bray Road.

Team captains on the day will be Michael Parkinson and Frank McKay, the chief executive of builders merchant Travis Perkins.

Most notable among the players will be former England cricket captain Michael Atherton, ex-Middlesex, Sussex and England man Ian Gould, and Hampshire's Ian Smith.

Ex-Crystal Palace and England footballer John Salako will be there with current Reading FC team-mate Adie Williams as will Cyrille Regis the ex-Coventry City player.

Channel4 cricket analyst Simon Hughes and British Airways chief executive Rod Eddington are also expected, as are TV's Carol Vorderman, Penny Smith and Mariella Frostrup.

Jamie Sears, chairman of the cricket club, which uses the weekend's profits to develop youth cricket, said: "It will be a really good fun day out for everybody.

"There will be a barbecue, face painting, a steel band, a raffle, a jazz band at the end of play, a Pimm's tent, ice creams, and of course lots of autographs. It is a big day and without it the club would not be here."

Michael Parkinson, one of Bray's famous residents, is hoping to maintain an impressive record of having beautiful weather on the day.

"We've never had a bad Sunday yet," he said.

He also paid tribute to his friends who have made the event such a success over the past quarter century, especially to the late Marion Montgomery, who died on

Monday last week, and her husband Laurie Holloway, who will be going ahead with his cabaret performance tonight (Friday).

Mr Parkinson said: "Marion was due to take part but that is sadly not possible.

"We shall remember Marion on the occasion.

"They have been a feature there and their contribution has been immeasurable.

"The fact we still have a club down there is due to people like Laurie, Marion, Rolf Harris and Sheila Ferguson, who have always been so supportive.

Mr Holloway said: "Marion would have wanted me to carry on."

■ Gates open for the cricket at 12.30pm on Sunday at Maidenhead and Bray Cricket Club. Entry is £5 for over 16s. Under 16s are free.

A Variety fund-raising concert.

TARBUCK'S THAMES BENEFIT!

It finally happened! After eight long months of careful planning, the long awaited evening with Jimmy Tarbuck and his friends was staged at the Richmond Theatre.

There's rarely been a Sunday evening like it! People flooded into the theatre from far and wide. Many were guests of some of the bigger companies and banks supporting the Thames Community Foundation. Others were individuals intent on an evening of fun and laughter.

Sandy Gilmour, director of the Foundation surpassed himself by drawing together a raffle to end all raffles. The Star prize was two return flights to Singapore, thanks to the generosity of Singapore Airlines. Perhaps the most amusing winner of a prize was Grant Gordon of William Grant & Sons - he won back the gallon of whisky he'd donated. This is now in the store cupboard for another event!

So, the stars were found, the programmes were produced and it was all set to go. One of the TCF Presidents, David Jacobs started the evening off and told the audience a little about the work of the Foundation. He then handed over to Jimmy Tarbuck who introduced Ronnie Corbett; Mike Yarwood; Kenny Lynch, Marion Montgomery and Laurie Holloway to do their bit.

left to right: Monica Unwin (TCF Vice-Chairman); Kenny Lynch; Marion Montgomery; Laurie Holloway; David Jacobs; Ronnie Corbett; Mike Yarwood and Jimmy Tarbuck

It was a spectacular evening of mirth and music! The jokes poured out, one after the other- it was a toss up as to whether the audience were enjoying it more than the comics or the other way around! Many laughed till they cried - the jokes punctuated only by the most marvellous jazz and blues music.

Unbelievably, the curtain finally dropped at 11.15pm. Jimmy, pleased at how well the evening had gone looked at Sandy Gilmour, and said "Do you want me to do another next year?" - well, what do you think Sandy said?!

This first venture earned the Foundation over £15,000. The wrinkles have now been ironed out and we are looking forward to even more next year.

Grateful thanks from everyone at the Thames Community Foundation go to Jimmy Tarbuck and his Friends.

A Royal Charity Varietry Show

Part One

GOD SAVE THE QUEEN

LAURIE HOLLOWAY ORCHESTRA — OVERTURE

PETER GORDENO DANCERS

TERRY WOGAN

RAY ALAN

DIANE SOLOMON

HOPE AND KEEN

CANTABILE

JACK AND SU DOUGLAS

DON MACLEAN

Interval

Part Two

PETER GORDENO AND DANCERS

BARBARA WINDSOR

ERNIE WISE

MARION MONTGOMERY

BERYL REID

PETER GORDENO

JIMMY LOGAN

TERRY WOGAN

PETER GORDENO DANCERS AND CAST

WENDY CRAIG

Jack Bentley was a trombonist who played in several big name bands – Jack Hylton, Ted heath, Geraldo and many others. He was also a member of the London Symphony Orchestra, that's how good he was.

He packed it all in and became the show business critic for the Sunday Mirror and he had his trombone made into a lamp standard. I knew him briefly. He died in 1994.

BBC Blogs

Wendy Craig

The reason I waffle on about Jack Bentley was that he married my dear friend Wendy Craig. Wendy is always invited by Maryann and me to our musical gatherings. She has two sons, one of which is a fine oboist, Alistair. He has long been principal oboe with the Birmingham Symphony Orchestra.

Alaster's daughter is Julia Bentley Dawkes who is a talented flautist. Music and talent runs through the family.

Julia, who is Wendy's granddaughter, is a trustee of the music trust which Marion and I set up in 1996. It is through Wendy's talent and Jack's musicality that has been passed on to their offspring.

Thank you, Wendy, for being a good friend to Maryann and me.

Some Photos From My Album

With Betty Boothroyd and Marion.

With Paul Anka.

With Bobby Davro.

With John Dankworth.   *A more youthful me with Gerry Lewis at Las Vegas Golf Course.*

With Kenny Lynch and John Conte.

Some More Lady Singers

✣ ✣✣✣✣✣✣✣✣✣✣✣✣✣✣✣✣✣✣

PATRICIA COOK

Patricia was beautiful and a singer. She was a friend of Don Black the songwriter. She told him that she was going to sing at a charity function over here in England and she was going to send for her pianist in the USA.

Don asked her why she was doing that when Laurie Holloway was already here and possibly one of the best accompanists in the world. (He modestly writes). I became Patricia's musical director and a friend of Edward.

Thanks to the Cooks' connections, Patricia was invited to sing at the White House in Washington DC. I was her accompanist.

Patricia Cook.

We did the gig and it was well received. In the audience was Sandra Day O'Connor who is a retired Associate Justice of the Supreme Court of the United States. She served from her 1981 appointment by President Ronald Reagan until her retirement in 2006. She was the first woman to serve on the Court.

During her time on the court, some publications ranked her among the most powerful women in the world. On August 12, 2009, she was awarded the Presidential Medal of Freedom by President Barack Obama. Mrs O'Connor invited Patricia and me to go with her to the Supreme Court and gave us a guided tour.

Fantastic!

✣ ✣✣✣✣✣✣✣✣✣✣✣✣✣✣✣✣✣✣

BARBARA STREISAND

My late wife, Marion and I had recently been married and we were appearing in New York at Basin Street East jazz club. A great venue and a great band.

Al Cohn was a member of the outfit and did some arranging for us.

We went after the show to eat at a hamburger joint and met Barbra Streisand's manager. He knew my work and asked me to be with her as she was coming to London to do Funny Girl.

Now between you and me, I didn't like Barbra Streisand's voice. You probably disagree, most people do, but that was the way I felt. I politely refused his request.

Her manager assured me that I wasn't being asked to be the pianist, but the musical director. I still refused.

Wind forward the clock, several years. I was a successful session pianist. You would be booked by a contractor to be at a certain studio on a certain day at a certain time.

One never knew who the artist would be.

Yes – you have guessed, this session the artist was Barbra Streisand. She of course didn't know a thing about my past feelings, and we got along quite well, in a tacet kind of way.

The album was her famous Christmas project which was a resounding success. I was paid £12 per session for it.

Serves me right!

✻ ✻✻✻✻✻✻✻✻✻✻✻✻✻✻✻✻✻

ELAINE PAIGE

I was Elaine's musical director for five years, probably lots more. Deke Arlon her manager asked me to help her with a new running order for a concert.

I did and we went on from there, doing lots of concerts and tours all over the place.

I often went to her house in Chelsea. A grand abode which I think was given to her as a farewell gift, by her previous boyfriend, Tim Rice.

She and I got along extremely well. One overseas date was at the Boston Pops in Boston, USA. We did tours of Scandinavia and many concerts in the UK.

Hampton Court was one of the big ones. We did lots of television appearances; we never stopped working.

Holloway in Hyde Park

MUSICIAN Laurie Holloway will be performing in front of thousands of people this weekend when he takes part in a three-night open air concert starring Sir Cliff Richard and Elaine Paige in London's Hyde Park.

Each Hyde Park concert will provide seating for 15,000 fans and Laurie, who has been Elaine Paige's musical director for 10 years, will be accompanying her during 10 of her best known hits such as 'Argentina', 'Memory' and 'I Know Him So Well'.

Laurie and Elaine last appeared in an open air festival at Hampton Court last summer and have just returned from a tour of Sweden. In October they are off to South Africa.

But on this occasion the Bray-based pianist didn't have so far to go to work – he has been rehearsing at Bray Studios!

July 16, 1999 - Windsor Observer

A concert with Elaine Paige and Sir Cliff Richard at Hyde Park.

In 1993 Elaine was asked to play Piaf the musical. I was the musical director.

I also had a small part on stage. My piano was towed on by an offstage person who wound a handle. I sat at the upright piano during this operation. One night I went all the way across by mistake at speed, scary.

Once on stage *Piaf*'s manager and I waited in silence for Piaf to show up, because she was always late.

I got fed up with the silence and started talking very quietly to the manager.

Sir Peter Hall was the director.

After one performance he gave all of us his notes.

He said that he noticed that I had started talking in the silent scene. I agreed that I had spoken. He said

"Don't."

I had been directed by the great Peter Hall.

My small band was terribly French sounding. I had Dave Richmond on bass, Chris Karan on drums, Kevin Street on accordion and Ronnie Price on electric piano. A first class band.

I took a week off to go to New York on the *QE2* and Ronnie Price was my understudy.

Elaine had begun to rely on me, so she took the week off as well.

Oh dear.

In 2002 I was the subject of *This Is Your Life*, the red book, and Elaine was a surprise guest and said some flattering comments about me.

She is lovely and I enjoyed my time as her musical director and friend.

Elaine Paige.

And Some More Male Singers

✳ ✳✳✳✳✳✳✳✳✳✳✳✳✳✳✳✳✳✳✳✳

BING CROSBY

As a session pianist I was very often engaged to play for famous singers.

I arrived at the studio one day to find that I was to accompany the great Bing Crosby.

Later, as he was passing the piano I said to him that if he would give me his autograph I would give him 3 strokes at golf.

He said "Three a side" meaning a hypothetical six strokes.

I agreed of course and got his autograph on the music I was playing for him.

It was "Autumn In New York" It is framed and hangs in my loo.

It was incidentally his last recording.

Soon after this date he went to play golf in Spain.

He died at La Morajela golf course, near Madrid, on the 14th of October 1977, from a heart attack.

Bing Crosby, 3 May 1903 – 14 October 1977.

✳ ✳✳✳✳✳✳✳✳✳✳✳✳✳✳✳✳✳✳✳

MANDY PATINKIN

At the time I wasn't too impressed, but I am now! I was asked to accompany a singer from the USA on the Gloria Hunniford radio show.

His name is Mandy Patinkin. A large man who looked as if he should be a bass baritone.

He wasn't. He sang with a falsetto voice.

I really enjoyed playing for him and we had a happy time together.

It was one of those brief but memorable musical experiences.

I thought that I would never see or hear of him again.

WRONG!

I watch him regularly on an American television series called *Homeland*.

He is a great actor.

I don't suppose anyone knows that he is also a very good singer with a falsetto voice.

Surprising.

✳✳✳✳✳✳✳✳✳✳✳✳✳✳✳✳✳✳✳

❊ ❊❊❊❊❊❊❊❊❊❊❊❊❊❊❊❊❊❊❊

LUCIANO PAVAROTTI

I was the musical director of the *Clive James* television show. Towards New Year's Eve, Maestro Pavarotti was engaged to talk on Clive's show and agreed that he would sing "Auld Lang Syne".

The problem was the expense of booking a full orchestra for one tune. I told them to leave it to me. I simulated every instrument on the keyboard in my studio so well that I fooled everybody.

Simulation sounds exactly that, and you can tell that it is electronic, but for some reason I had cracked it. "Auld Lang Syne" sounded as if it was being played by a genuine orchestra. Would Maestro Pavarotti agree? Well he did.

He sang along to my track, phonetically of course, and was blissfully unaware that he was being accompanied by my electronic synthesizer. He thanked me and he even signed the music for me.

It hangs with all my other mementoes, in my loo.

❊ ❊❊❊❊❊❊❊❊❊❊❊❊❊❊❊❊❊❊❊

BOB MONKHOUSE

One of the easiest jobs I ever had was being the pianist for Bob Monkhouse. We would travel in his big American car to gigs. I would play him on with some bright tune. I would sit there and laugh at his jokes. Twice, because there was always a punch line at the end of the story.

At the end of his act he would sing a bawdy song to my accompaniment. That was it. An easy gig.

I made two videos with him. He and I composed the songs for the shows. One was called "Bob Monkhouse Exposes Himself ". I forget what the other was called. We made them at the Lakeside Country Club in Frimley Green.

His act was definitely parental guidance recommended. Very clever but quite near the bone.

British Comedy Guide

Bob Monkhouse,
1 June 1928 – 29 December 2003.

I have in my old diary of 1957-ish, an entry which says "Bob Monkhouse, Blackpool, £5". £5 in those days would be worth at least £6 today.*

I remember doing a gig with him where we stayed overnight in a hotel. We shared a room. I went to bed early just in case he wanted to talk and tell more jokes.

He came to my house for dinner with the then-deputy Prime Minister John Prescott and his lovely wife Pauline. He was quite posh and lived in Saint John's Wood.

I believe that he was a part of a family who made a fortune from a well-known biscuit brand.

Not a bundle of laughs until he did his act. Then he was.

More memories.

**About £100 today.*

Clubs, Nightclubs and Theatres

✳ ✳✳✳✳✳✳✳✳✳✳✳✳✳✳✳✳✳✳✳✳

Let me tell you about my experiences in various nightspots throughout my career. I suppose my first venture into clubland was when I first arrived in London from my northern roots and went to Ronnie Scott's jazz club in what is now Chinatown.

I also often went to a club in Old Compton Street called The Downbeat club owned by two great musicians, Mike Senn and Jackie Sharp. I was playing piano in a ballroom called the Astoria in Charing Cross Road and in between sessions I used to go to these two clubs to hear the wonderful music played by legendary jazz musicians. Eddie Thompson was the resident pianist at the Downbeat Club and Ronnie Scott had the greats like Ella Fitzgerald and Oscar Peterson. I was in jazz heaven. Ronnie's moved from Chinatown to its permanent site in Frith Street. It became virtually my home address!

I was, as I've said, playing in the Astoria ballroom which meant playing for a tea dance in the afternoon from 2.30 pm and then proper dancing in the evening. There were two bands with the celebrated revolving stage. I finished my set at 10.30 pm but the clock was always 5 minutes fast so I finished at 10.25 pm. I was offered a permanent job around the corner in Meard Street at the Gargoyle Club. On finding out that it was only five minutes away and started at 10.30 pm I accepted it! That meant that I was playing the piano from 2.30 in the afternoon until 3.15 in the morning. I learned a lot of tunes

The Gargoyle was a sophisticated strip club. I didn't only learn tunes, I also learned quite a bit about life!

My first experience of the proper "up north" clubs came when I was musical director for Cleo Laine.

She was the singer in her husband John Dankworth's band but had just recorded a hit record called "If We Lived On Top Of A Mountain". This meant that when she chose to go on the road as a solo star, I was recruited as her pianist/musical director. We would perform two different clubs each night in the same area. The bass player and drummer were local semi-professional men that were resident in each club. They had proper jobs during the day. The standard of their playing was always good enough for me to knock them into shape. After all it wasn't brain surgery. John occasionally turned up and the place became electric.

Discogs

Cleo Laine

After a while Cleo decided to go back to John's band on a regular basis. Dudley Moore had just left to do bigger things in a different direction and I achieved my long-standing ambition to be in a fantastic jazz band. I had a wonderful time, just sitting at the piano listening to the wonderful arrangements by John and Dave Lindup. I suppose I played my part in the band but the thrill for me was just being a part of it. So I achieved two ambitions. Being in the John Dankworth band and also appearing at Ronnie Scott's club.

As prevously mentioned, from 1970 to 1975 1 was the musical director for Engelbert Humperdinck. Quite a career change. We appeared all over the USA in what were night spots or theatres. We spent one month every year in Las Vegas at the Riviera Hotel. Fortunately none of us were gamblers. The rest of the time was spent doing weeks in various cities. On Monday afternoon we would rehearse the orchestra that each venue provided. It comprised 4 trumpets, 4 trombones, woodwind, percussion and a pianist. I didn't play because I was conducting. We had our own rhythm section of guitar, bass guitar and drums.

We would spend most daylight hours playing golf, do the show in the evening, have a get-together later in the bar and then travel to the next city on each Sunday. In the UK we also appeared at various places. We did the London Palladium a few times and also Batley Variety Club. Batley was a very famous venue that every top name played. It was packed every night because it was a good old-fashioned northern club that wasn't terribly expensive for the audience. Our drummer, John Spooner, and I sought out the nearest golf course and we played often during the week at Moor Allerton.

We met the professional there who was the wonderful Peter Alliss. My time with Engelbert was non-educational but great fun.

❀❀❀❀❀❀❀❀❀❀❀❀❀❀❀❀❀❀

THE COOL ELEPHANT

The cabaret was mainly American stars. They normally did a two-week stint.

Names such as Mel Tormé, June Christie, Oscar Brown Jr, and a new American lady who had just had a hit record singing "When Sunny Gets Blue". She was called Marion Montgomery.

Abigail Ann Montgomery Holloway

She was a tasty bird. I fancied her and plucked up the courage to ask if I could take her home. She agreed and told me that Dudley Moore had asked the same thing but as I asked first she would go with me.

We left the club, in Margaret Street, after the festivities and discovered that it was pouring down.

I was driving an MG midget and the top was down.

This American star was obliged to wait in the rain until I had put the lid on the car, and while I was doing this, Dudley drove by in his Rolls Royce.

I suggested that she had made a mistake, but we had a laugh and I took her back to her hotel – it was only 100 yards away round the corner!

I got a peck on the cheek and hoped for better things later. Our daughter is called Abigail!

❀❀❀❀❀❀❀❀❀❀❀❀❀❀❀❀❀❀

✳ ✳✳✳✳✳✳✳✳✳✳✳✳✳✳✳✳✳✳✳✳

JOHN DANKWORTH AND CLEO LAINE

This could be a long story. John and Cleo were my dear friends. John has died but Cleo thankfully is still with us.

I was playing the piano at the Adelphi theatre in London's Strand. The show was Lionel Bart's *Blitz!*.

John Dankworth,
20 September 1927 – 6 February 2010.

I got a call from my agent, Dick Katz, asking me if I would go to Southampton to do a gig with John Dankworth and Cleo Laine. Their pianist couldn't be with them on this occasion. Can a duck swim?

I immediately got a deputy for my night away from *Blitz!* and went to meet and play for my idols. It's all a bit of a blur but I must have done ok because they seemed pleased with my playing.

Cleo was at the time the singer in John's band. She had recorded a single which was quite a hit, called *"If We Lived On Top Of A Mountain"*.

She had to leave John's band and go solo to promote the song and also to be a soloist.

I was asked to be her pianist/musical director. I jumped at it. We did clubs, all over, two a night, and became very good friends. John would turn up occasionally and made the gig even better.

I would use the bass player and drummer from the club where we were appearing. Some were ok and some were terrible. That didn't matter, there was always Cleo and me.

The pianist in John's band was the wonderful Dudley Moore. A brilliant pianist. After a while he left to join Peter Cook and became even more famous.

There was a spell where the pianist with John was Alan Branscombe, a brilliant all round musician. Unfortunately he was dependant on drugs and that eventually was his downfall.

Cleo had rejoined John's band and I was invited to be John's pianist. I was ecstatic and I had a memorable time, playing alongside fabulous jazz musicians; playing John and David Lindup's great arrangements and I had a wonderful time.

We made several recordings and actually recorded one of my compositions, "Holloway House".

John was asked to provide the music for a new sophisticated club in Margaret Street, London. It was called The Cool Elephant. The music was the John Dankworth sextet, John, Art Elefson, Johnny Marshall, Spike Heatley, Allan Ganley and me.

The other group was (you won't believe this) the Dudley Moore trio.

Peter McGurk on bass and Chris Karan on drums.

Fantastic. What a life.

We played our own sets and accompanied American stars such as Mel Tormé, June Christie, Oscar Brown Junior and Marion Montgomery.

The clientele was quite sophisticated. People like David Frost, Jeanette Scott, who eventually married Mel Tormé, and where I first met Princess Margaret.

The club eventually closed. We weren't as popular as Ronnie Scott's.

John and Cleo lived near Milton Keynes and my wife and I were regular visitors to their dinner parties.

We were invited once and told to bring a shovel. For what?

They wanted a swimming pool and we were expected to help with the excavation.

I recorded several albums with Cleo. I was the producer, arranger and pianist. We recorded one album of the music of Frank Loesser. His wife was known as the evil of two Loessers.

John and Cleo were good friends of Princess Margaret and she often was there enjoying the music, smoking and imbibing whisky and water. She later was a regular guest at my house.

John became Sir John and Cleo became Dame Cleo. Well deserved.

They had a stable block which they turned into a theatre. Marion and I were regular performers. They eventually built a proper theatre and still called it The Stables.

In the foyer are six large glass images depicting their friends. Marion and I are immortally there.

When John was very ill, he went to hospital and I became the musical director and conductor of a gala night at The Stables theatre.

❋❋❋❋❋❋❋❋❋❋❋❋❋❋❋❋❋❋❋

During the rehearsal Cleo and family were called to the hospital because John had relapsed.

Cleo and family returned to the theatre and told us in the dressing room that John had died.

She said that the show must go on. The audience wouldn't knoq until later in the show when announced that John had died. I will never forget the sound emotion that the audience made and transmitted. It was a sound that will live in my head for ever.

I wrote songs with Sir John, I became one of his best friends, I played the piano for him when there was just him and me in the room. I miss him.

I see Cleo fairly often. The last time was a lovely lunch at her house with Jacqui her daughter.

She still has her infectious laugh. We go back a long way.

Sir John and Dame Cleo, happy memories.

A kind letter to me from John..

Celebration special

By Clare Brotherwood

A HANDFUL of locals played a large part in an event to help Dame Cleo Laine and John Dankworth celebrate 50 years in showbusiness last weekend.

Arguably showbusiness's most famous couple, Dame Cleo and her husband ended the weekend with a special 'Concert of a Lifetime' at London's Royal Albert Hall.

But 'Cleo and John's Golden Music Jubilee' had begun the night before at The Stables, their own theatre at Wavendon near Milton Keynes, with a concert headed by the undisputed star of the show, pianist Laurie Holloway.

The show was to have been headlined by Laurie and his wife, Marion Montgomery -- whose portraits are etched in glass alongside Cleo and John's in the theatre's foyer.

But Marion died of cancer in July and John Dankworth told a packed house: "This is the beginning of our big weekend. We decided it should just be a wonderful musical weekend, and there was no question who we wanted to celebrate with us - our soulmates and co-founders, Laurie Holloway and his lovely wife Marion Montgomery.

"But when Marion lost her courageous battle we felt the only thing to do was to give over the whole show to Laurie in celebration of Marion's life."

The Dankworths have known Laurie since 1962 when he went on the road with Cleo for two years before joining the John Dankworth Orchestra. And introducing him, John continued: "He is one of my favourite people and my favourite musician. If I had not been myself the person I would really like to be is Laurie Holloway. He is the consummate musician."

Laurie, who lives in Bray, wasn't the only local on the bill, for alongside what John Dankworth called 'a couple of interlopers' (he played 'I'm Old Fashioned' on the clarinet and Dame Cleo ended the show with 'I've Got a Crush on You') were three singers who have benefitted from working with The Montgomery Holloway Music Trust – set up to give aspiring singers and musicians the chance to learn from and perform with professionals. They included Jemima Olchawski, 18, from Ascot, and former Brigidine School pupil, Liz Hunter, 26,

■ CELEBRATING 50 YEARS IN SHOWBUSINESS: Dame Cleo Laine and John Dankworth.

who lives in Maidenhead.

Jemima, a pupil at Charters School, Sunningdale and a member of the Charters Youth and Community Centre until she went to Jesus College, Oxford to study philosophy and politics, sang 'My Baby Cares for Me', while Liz Hunter, who recently appeared with Laurie in Slough's first outdoor jazz festival, 'Jazz on the Lawn' at the Observer's Upton Court head quarters, sang her own composition, 'Contradictions of the Heart'.

Liz tours the country with her own jazz band, Anything Goes, and this year released her first CD, but she said afterwards: "I feel really honoured, especially as it was in memory of Marion - and then to have chosen a song I had written!"

Others taking part were the winner and runner up of the Marion Montgomery Jazz Divas Awards, who were chosen last month at the Isle of Wight Jazz Festival, and Cleo and John's daughter, Jacqueline Dankworth - a tutor at the MHMT seminars, while the whole show was linked by Laurie and Marion's daughter, Abigail, another ex-Brigidine School pupil, who related the story of how her parents met, when Laurie was a member of the John Dankworth Sextet, before explaining the work of the MHMT and how it has involved more than 300 musicians and singers since it was founded six years ago.

■ LAURIE HOLLOWAY: Star of the show.

The weekend wasn't just a good one for Cleo and John – the night before Wavendon, Laurie, who is musical director on BBC TV's 'Parkinson' show, had been guest pianist with the BBC Concert Orchestra in a live recording of Radio 2's 'Friday Night is Music Night', when he performed his own arrangements of 'Blue Skies', 'Beatles Bonanza' and 'Love for Sale' with 60 musicians!

■ 'Cleo Laine, John Dankworth and Friends' star at the Wycombe Swan, High Wycombe on Sunday, November 3 at 7.30pm. Tickets are priced from £14.50 to £18.50. Booking and info: 01494 512000.

✳ ✳✳✳✳✳✳✳✳✳✳✳✳✳✳✳✳✳✳✳

I Was Judy Garland's Piano Player: The Story Behind Her Triumphant London Palladium Shows

An article by Martin Chilton

Judy Garland's wretched final months in London in 1969, when she was giving chaotic nightclub performances, are explored in the new biopic Judy, starring Renée Zellweger. But just five years before those disastrous shows, London had been a much happier place for the actress and singer. She received standing ovations, was mobbed by fans, and went out in the town with a glitzy new social circle. For the first time in ages, she seemed happy.

Judy Garland, 10 June 1922 – 22 June 1969.

Laurie Holloway, who was the musical director of the Michael Parkinson show and the first three series of *Strictly Come Dancing*, saw the light-hearted and merry side of Garland from close quarters during this period, when he was hired to be her musical director and pianist for nearly six weeks of rehearsals and two sell-out Palladium shows in November 1964.

Holloway, 81, who also went on to write the theme tunes for *Blind Date* and *Game for a Laugh*, and who has accompanied leading musicians such as Ella Fitzgerald, Val Doonican and Mel Tormé, was a jobbing pianist at the time he got the call to work with 42-year-old Garland.

The *Wizard of Oz* star was first brought to the UK in 1951 by the powerful talent agent Harold Davison. "My agent Dick Katz worked for them, and even though I was young, just 25 at the time, they thought I would be a good fit to be Judy Garland's piano player for one season," Holloway tells me. "When we discussed it, they asked me if I would like to help Judy and her 18-year-old daughter Liza Minnelli prepare for a concert at the London Palladium. So I spent about six weeks with the two of them, although it was mainly with Judy."

The concerts were announced on October 10 but the clamour for tickets to see Garland – who had even outshone the Beatles at a special 'Night of 100 Stars' charity event at the London Palladium three months before – was so frenzied that the concert sold out even before the advertisements appeared in that evening's newspapers. A second concert for November was immediately scheduled.

Garland had not been in great shape earlier in 1964. She had collapsed in Hong Kong and was later admitted to a London hospital for treatment on wounds on her wrists. Few believed claims that she had accidentally cut herself opening a trunk bound with metal.

Judy Garland on stage at the London Palladium with Laurie Holloway accompanying, 1964: Getty

By the time she met up with Holloway, though, she was in a far better place mentally and physically.

She was living in a large rented house in Chelsea and was finding ways to relax ("I bake myself a chicken pie," she told reporters) and was a regular on the London social scene. In October, she visited singer Annie Ross's club Annie's Room in Covent Garden; she attended the opening night of the celebrated production of *Hay Fever* at the National Theatre, a play written by her friend Noël Coward and starring Edith Evans and Derek Jacobi; she saw Dame Margot Fonteyn dance in *Giselle* at the Royal Opera House.

Liza Minelli and Judy Garland on stage.

Holloway remembers this hectic time fondly. "We worked a bit in the daytime and in the evening we would go out all the time, mainly to entertainer Danny La Rue's nightclub, which was a revue club in Hanover Square. One of the artists there at the time was Ronnie Corbett. He told me he hated it when Judy walked in, because everybody looked at her instead of watching the cabaret."

Garland, who had recorded a new EP for Capitol Records earlier that summer, was interested in honing the set-lists for the Palladium concerts. Holloway says they spent a lot of time discussing which songs to include in the shows. "We talked a lot about music together. We chatted about what things in her repertoire would be good," says Holloway.

Garland was using an orchestra conducted by Harry Robinson for the shows but was keen to involve Holloway. One of the tunes they settled on was an intimate piano-based version of Just in Time, a song which had been a hit for Peggy Lee, Blossom Dearie and Frank Sinatra. "I would get to the big house in Chelsea she was renting late in the morning and then she would come down and be cheery," recalls Holloway. "She was married at the time to a gay guy called Mark Herron. Liza was about 18, and she had boyfriends. We just used to hang out, laugh and practice. We did not have to rehearse too much, because they knew what they were doing anyway. Judy was in a good mood at that time, probably because she was working with Liza, so she had to behave herself."

Garland had played a month-long residency at the Palladium in 1951 and told friends she was looking forward to returning to a place that was full of nostalgia and where she felt "that I'm home". The first concert, on November 8, began at 8pm. The second, on the following Wednesday, was moved to a later midnight start. "The reason that show was so late at night is that so many other entertainers wanted to come and see the show," explains Holloway, "so we started after they had all finished their gigs."

The concerts, which were filmed by ITV and later released as an album that reached No41 on the Billboard charts, were each more than two hours long, with Holloway playing a grand piano near the front of the vast stage. "I was on piano, slap bang in the middle of the front and at one point Judy came and sat on my piano stool and I accompanied her singing a couple of songs. We had worked out that routine for a couple of numbers during the rehearsals in Chelsea. After one song sitting on the stool, she kissed me. At the end of the show, when I went out of the stage door, all the girls wanted to kiss me just because Judy had."

With Liza Minnelli in recent years.

The set-lists included versions of "Hello, Dolly", "Don't Rain On My Parade" and, of course, "Over the Rainbow", the beautiful ballad composed by Harold Arlen and Yip Harburg that had provided such an iconic moment in The Wizard of Oz and which became Garland's signature song.

Her daughter also sang solo songs, duets and joined in the banter, joking about her mother's "rainbow fetish".

Holloway, who would later accompany Minnelli as the pianist on solo gigs in England, witnessed the mother-daughter dynamic close-up. "Liza overdid it a bit and Judy had to slap her down musically now and again," Holloway says. "Liza was

trying to impress but Judy just came on and did her bit. Liza has always been like that, slightly over the top."

Holloway believes that the purity of Garland's vocals was enough to electrify the London crowd. "With Judy, so much emotion came from the audience. When we did the overture, which was about six or seven minutes long and which included *Over the Rainbow,* the hairs on the back of my neck stood up.

She wasn't the greatest singer but she was so emotional – a bit like Shirley Bassey or Dorothy Squires. They lived their songs and put everything into them, rather than just delivering a story."

Liza Minnelli performing with her mother Judy Garland at the Palladium.

After the Palladium shows, Garland remained in London for a couple of months. She was a judge on an episode of the television show *Juke Box Jury* and attended a special event with her fan club at the Hotel Russell in London. She even made plans to remain in the UK and make a film of the stage play Laurette. In the end, she returned to America – and her decline began in earnest.

Judy Garland and her partner Mark Herron at the Palladium, 1964.

Getty

Garland once told a young Barbara Streisand, "don't let them do to you what they did to me". It is hard not to be moved by some of the pitiful elements of her life and what the exploitative men in the entertainment business did to her. From a young age, studio bosses popped uppers and downers in her mouth. Garland ended up suffering from hepatitis, exhaustion, kidney ailments, nervous breakdowns, oscillating weight problems, self-harming, injuries from falls and drug addiction. "Sometimes I feel like I'm living in a blizzard," she said. "An absolute blizzard."

By the time Garland returned to London in late 1968, her situation was probably beyond rescue. She was booked for a five-week cabaret spot at The Talk of the Town, next to Leicester Square. She was about to marry her fifth husband, Mickey Deans (played by Finn Wittrock in *Judy*). She was drinking heavily, taking drugs, slurring her words and looking haggard. She was desperate for cash. Due to mismanagement and embezzlement, she owed hundreds of thousands of dollars in back taxes in America.

The London shows were a disaster. One evening in January 1969, after she had kept the crowd waiting for 80 minutes, she was heckled and booed. Some cruel members of the audience even hurled bread rolls and glasses at her. She left the stage after three songs. The acclaim of the Palladium seemed a lifetime away.

On June 22 1969, she died at her Belgravia home from an accidental "incautious self-overdosage" of the sleeping tablets she had taken since she was a child. Zellweger's biopic – and a new documentary called Sid & Judy, which is narrated by Jennifer Jason Leigh and Jon Hamm – will simply add to the heart-breaking legend.

Fifty years after her death, however, some prefer to remember Garland as the talented actress who blew audiences away in *The Wizard of Oz* – and went on to make classics such as *Meet Me in St Louis, Judgment at Nuremberg* and *A Star Is Born* – and as the singer who delighted audiences around the world for 20 years.

"Judy had an unbelievable aura on stage and she was a fun lady and really, really nice person to work with back in 1964," says Holloway. "I didn't work with Judy later on, when she became a bit difficult, and I am glad I didn't. I saw the good times."

❊ JOOLS AND LIZA ❊

I was doing the Bruce Forsyth special when there was a knock on my dressing room door. I opened it to find Jools Holland with Liza Minelli.

They needed my assistance. Jools was going to play a piece which I had previously played for Liza. Jools found it rather difficult to read the music. I explained what Liza wanted and off they went.

Always willing to oblige – even the opposition.

✳ ✳✳✳✳✳✳✳✳✳✳✳✳✳✳✳✳✳✳✳✳

A POEM BY BENNY GREEN

With Benny Green and his wife, Toni Kanal.

An Impenitent Musician

I can not drive, I can not dance,
I can not give a name to plants,
I can not paint, I can not plumb,
I can not gauge by rule of thumb,
I can not build, or read a map,
I can not stop a dripping tap,
I can not mend a silly fuse,
but I can sing a twelve bar blues.

I do not smoke, I hardly drink,
I often find it hard to think,
I can not dive, I barely swim,
I will not jog, I will not slim,
I do not bet, I can not skate,
There is no captain of my fate,
but one thing can be said for me
I know the whole of "Cherokee".

I can not mime a single thing,
and I don't know Limoges from Ming,
I do not know the rules of chess,
but I am a bit careful in my dress,
I don't play bridge, or golf, or squash,
I do not talk particularly posh,
I could not quote you "Much Ado"
but I can busk "I Cried For You".

I can't retain a single date,
I can't invent, I can't create,
I do not know the names of trees,
or what impels the birds and bees.
I can't subtract, I can't divide,
and muddle Jekyll up with Hyde,
yet I recall when I first knew …
"There'll Never Ever Be Another You".

Some Personalities

❄ ❄❄❄❄❄❄❄❄❄❄❄❄❄❄❄❄❄❄

DAVID JACOBS

A short story regarding David Jacobs. I was playing piano on the David Jacobs television series at Rediffusion, Wembley.

That was where London Weekend Television started and I was heavily involved in the orchestra under the musical director, Harry Rabinowitz.

One day I was walking down Sloane Street in Chelsea when I saw approaching me, David Jacobs and another gentleman.

David said "Hello Laurie. Have you met the King of Spain?"

David Jacobs CBE, 19 May 1926 – 2 September 2013.

❄❄❄❄❄❄❄❄❄❄❄❄❄❄❄❄❄❄

MICHEL ROUX

I am a piano player who likes to cook. It relaxes me and demands my total concentration. But I cheat.

A good friend of mine, the late Michel Roux, was one of the finest chefs in the whole world.

He suggested the I get a Thermomix® which does most of the cooking for you. Who am I to disagree with the top chef in the world, with a 3-Michelin-Star restaurant called The Waterside, in my own village? His lady is Amanda Gilliland. She is my friend and my doctor. She and Michel lived next to the famous restaurant. Anyway, she bought for me a Thermomix.

My wife, Maryann, and I, were invited to dine with Amanda and Monsieur Roux at their house in Bray. I was asked to provide the starter. Me, the piano player. I decided to make Gazpacho soup. My friend, Michel Roux thought it was very good and tasteful. Me, the piano player and cook.

I was now a trifle cocky and invited Michel and Amanda to our house where Maryann and I would prepare dinner for all of us. I was to make fish pie. I of course used the Thermomix which Amanda had given to me. Michel said that he liked my cooking. I was overjoyed.

Never mind that I was musical director of the top television shows, Michel Roux liked my cooking! Michel opened a fine bistro near where Maryann and I live. Each Christmas I play carols and Christmas songs, Michel reciting a humorous story.

Michel died early in 2020. He was a charming gentleman and Maryann and I miss him very much.

As he liked my cooking, perhaps I could get a job at Michel's bistro if I ever give up playing the piano.

❄❄❄❄❄❄❄❄❄❄❄❄❄❄❄❄❄❄

❄❄❄❄❄❄❄❄❄❄❄❄❄❄❄❄❄❄

GEORGE BEST

George Best was 50 years old when a television company decided to get his friends together for an early morning live programme. I remember that along with George was the footballer Ian Callaghan, Michael Parkinson. Kenny Lynch, me and others I can't remember.

It was extremely early in the morning and I probably had had a late night previously.

When we got to the studio there were only flasks of disgusting black coffee to drink. I drank lots to get me in gear.

After a short time I felt the effects of the caffeine and started to shake.

I managed to play the piano for a song sung by Kenny Lynch but I was in a very hyper state of caffeine overdose.

At the end of the programme it had been agreed that we would all go to the canteen for a good old fry up.

I had to decline as I wouldn't have been able to hold a knife and fork without shaking.

I missed that lads' get together, but made up for it many times later.

❄❄❄❄❄❄❄❄❄❄❄❄❄❄❄❄❄❄

STIRLING MOSS

I was in Monte Carlo with my wife Marion. We were invited by our friends Martin and Patti Hone. Martin was very well connected to the motor racing fraternity. In fact he owned a jazz club in Birmingham called The Opposite Lock Club. Opposite lock of course being a motor racing expression. Other guests in Monte Carlo were Sir Stirling and Lady Susie Moss.

Stirling had been a Grand Prix winner at the Monte Carlo round the houses race. He asked me if I would l would like him to drive me around the course.

Can a duck swim?

It was fantastic to be driven round the scene of his former triumph by the world's most famous racing driver.

Of course we didn't go round at his racing speed but we still went fairly quickly.

Another wonderful memory.

With Sir Stirling and Lady Moss.

❄❄❄❄❄❄❄❄❄❄❄❄❄❄❄❄❄❄

✳✳✳✳✳✳✳✳✳✳✳✳✳✳✳✳✳✳✳

KENNY LYNCH

Someone once said that Kenny Lynch and Laurie Holloway are joined at the hip. Kenny and I were friends for in excess of 50 years.

We first met in Las Vegas when I was with Humperdinck and Kenny was visiting with loads of his friends.

Kenneth Lynch OBE,
18 March 1938 – 18 December 2019.

He had many friends. I think that everybody in "the business" knew Kenny.

We found that we liked the same kind of music and we started to do concerts with my trio.

He had a tremendous repertoire and I learned a lot of great songs from him. His favourite titles were from the American songbook.

Kenny lived in a cottage in the depths of the country, but we always rehearsed at my house. I've just realised why, I had a piano and he didn't.

We made an album called *After Dark* which is one happy recording. I'll tell you about another album later. He was not the greatest time keeper.

There was a concert where he turned up as I was playing my last solo. One couldn't be annoyed with him, well you could, but within a few minutes it was all forgotten.

He was a poor car driver. He told the story about driving up the M40 having smoked a joint. He was going far too slowly because he couldn't put his foot on the accelerator. He was pulled over by the police, they asked him why he was going so slowly.

He said that he was saving petrol!

We played a lot of golf together, and were both members of Temple golf club. We had similar handicaps and enjoyed our friendship on the golf course.

There was a time when he had been banned from driving, so he organised his local bus to drop him off at the golf course gates. He certainly had a way with him.

He was a good friend of Jimmy Tarbuck and they worked together many times. Kenny and I were often asked to do our show at Nick Parkinson's hostelry, the Royal Oak, Paley Street. We were very popular there.

I tried to get annoyed with him at one concert. He took a break in the middle of the show and said it was time for everyone to have a comfort break. I had to play while everyone got up to go to the loo.

I was not amused.

Let me tell you about the second album. My trio and I recorded the backing tracks in my studio with Kenny putting his voice on later. The tracks included my arrangement of the *Soliloquy* from *Carousel*.

We went to Pete Brown's studio in the country to put his voice on. He sang it wonderfully.

Kenny wasn't well and every time I saw him, he looked dreadful.

But we finished the album.

Soon after, his lady Julie called me early one morning to tell me that my dear friend, Kenny, had died.

The album, when it is released, will be a testament to his talent and strength during his illness.

He was buried in Nettlebed, his local village. We gave him a good send off on a damp and cold day.

Jimmy Tarbuck gave a lovely eulogy to the "late" Kenny Lynch in the church. Thank you Kenny, for your musicality and your friendship.

I'll miss him for a long time, like forever.

With Dave Olney, left, and Harold Fisher - my Trio.

Radio

✤✤✤✤✤✤✤✤✤✤✤✤✤✤✤✤✤✤

MRS MILLS

My first meeting with Gordon Mills was in about 1961. I have a vivid recollection of the circumstances.

Johnny Gray and His Band of The Day was asked to do a radio series called Mrs Mills And Her Mates.

The idea was that Glad, or Gladys, (Mrs Mills and no relation to Gordon) was the hostess of the show and each week she was joined by us (the Band Of Decay) and a harmonica-playing-singing group called The Viscounts.

It was a supremely happy series due to the wonderful Mrs Mills.

Gladys Mills 29 August 1918 – 24 February 1978.

She played and laughed her way through each week's show. Never have I met a happier, more soul-lifting lady and I forget how long the series ran - probably about 13 weeks.

Of the three Viscounts, Gordon Mills was one and in dire contrast to the wonderful Mrs Mills they were the most disenchanted, argumentative and unhappy trio perhaps ever assembled.

C'est la vie.

✤✤✤✤✤✤✤✤✤✤✤✤✤✤✤✤✤

"AT THE PIANO"

From July 1984 to July 1991 I made 14 BBC radio broadcasts called *At The Piano*.

When I was a kid, I used to listen to Semprini doing a similar thing. I never dreamed that one day I would be called upon to do the same, play solo piano.

Each programme was for 15 minutes. No interruptions, only the front and back announcements that it was me. I played anything I wanted, mostly the American songbook. Well-known tunes in my style, whatever that is.

Eventually I was not invited to record any more because the mood had changed.

No more "good" music, plenty of records of a different kind of music. It would be churlish of me to say that most of it is rubbish.

But I will be churlish.

✤ REGARDING "AT THE PIANO" ✤

Once I was given the chance to record at the concert hall of Broadcasting House. It was wrong! No intimacy of a small room. Never again I said.

DAME EDNA EVERAGE

I have been the musical director for Dame Edna Everage, alias Barry Humphries, from about 1983 to the present day. We have done countless television series together and many private functions.

He calls my orchestra "Laurie Holloway and the Hollowtones."

The television series we have made are: *An audience with Dame Edna Everage, One more audience with Dame Edna Everage, A night on Mount Edna, Dame Edna's Neighbourhood Watch* and *Dame Edna's Work Experience.* Recently we did *Dame Edna Rules The Waves.* It was set on a fictional boat called *The Ocean Widow.*

I've done lots of arrangements for her/him and we have become great friends. We've composed many tunes together, most of them bawdy and full of innuendos.

Sometimes Barry appears as Sir Les Patterson and is intentionally quite revolting. Sir Les and I performed at the Whitehall Theatre in London for a week.

With Sir Les Patterson.

He wore a pipe down his trousers to emphasise his size. He said "I know what you ladies are looking at. You're looking at my penis. And here he is, Laurie Holloway, my fine upstanding pianist."

But back to Edna.

On the occasions when we travel to concerts, I address him naturally as Barry. When we get there, and he starts to get dressed he becomes Edna.

Edna once said that she hadn't seen me for such a long time. We had just driven together to the concert but now she had changed personality into Dame Edna. I actually averted my eyes when Edna started to put on her frock.

Edna was a favourite of Michael Parkinson and she always gave her Christmas message on the show. Always hilarious.

Patricia Emily Perry, 28 June 1907 – 19 February 2008.

She was invited to be a guest on Michael's last show. Barry called me to ask what I thought Edna should sing.

I thought about it and called him back to say that Edna should sing *"The Parky's Over"* to the tune of *"The Party's Over".*

I even made a demo recording of me singing it in an Edna voice. Quite a collector's item.

Edna always had her bridesmaid Madge Allsop on the show. Madge never smiled and never said a word. At her audition she said nothing and did nothing. She said that's why she got the job.

Madge was a lovely lady whose real name was Emily Perry. Emily died in 2008. This was acknowledged in the recent television special, *Dame Edna Rules The Waves.* I carried the pseudo ashes in an urn to Edna who threw it through the porthole to a pseudo-watery grave.

Dear Madge was replaced by her "sister" Mabel. Another bundle of laughs.

Barry is married to the gorgeous Lizzie Spender, his fourth wife. Lizzie is the daughter of Sir Stephen Spender, the poet.

I've had a marvellous time being associated with Barry Humphries. Long may it continue.

Some Songwriters

✳✳✳✳✳✳✳✳✳✳✳✳✳✳✳✳✳✳✳✳

ANTHONY NEWLEY

I was the pianist/musical director for Anthony Newley. I think the year was about 1959 when I lived in the caravan at Haringey.

I don't know how it happened but Anthony Newley somehow got the garage number.

He called and asked if I could help him with a rehearsal and possibly go on the road with him.

I was absolutely thrilled. It is all a bit of a blur but I remember going to his apartment and rehearsing with him and then going on the road with him to various venues.

At the time he was prolific writer and actor.

He was writing with Leslie Bricusse, I was most envious. The right place at the wrong time.

But I suppose my time was to come.

Many years later I was the musical director of a television show celebrating 50 years after World War 2.

I was asked to go to Tony's home because he was involved in the show. He was living with his

Anthony Newley,
24 September 1931 – 14 April 1999.

mother. This superstar who had been on top of the world, married to beautiful women, was now a virtual recluse.

We worked on two numbers for the television show and he was wonderful. I still have the tape recordings of our rehearsals.

So I first worked with Anthony when I was a young and ambitious piano player and now working with him as an established musical director and he was fading from his past glory, but still wonderful.

The last time I worked with him was on a television special. He sang *"Sweet Gingerbread Man"* which he had written.

More happy memories.

BURT BACHARACH

In my studio session days I was asked to play the piano on a Burt Bacharach film recording session. It was *Casino Royal*, the James Bond film. The year was 1967.

All studio freelance session players were properly and smartly dressed. Jacket and tie always.

We were shocked when Mr Bacharach turned up to conduct us in an open neck shirt and tennis shoes. He was so loose and relaxed that I suppose we followed his lead.

I love his music. I think that he is a modern George Gershwin.

Unexpected twists of melody. Great lyrics usually by Hal David. He is very talented.

On this particular film recording session he had his wife, Angie Dickenson the actress and his second of four wives, in the recording booth.

I suppose that she was there to keep him company and to tell him how good he was. After each "take" he would turn around to her and blow her a kiss. How soppy! But it was good music.

For some reason known only to himself, there were five pianists playing five grand pianos, all playing the same music at the same time. Why I don't know.

By the way I am the only one of the five still alive. A clean healthy life! Who's kidding who?

❉❉❉❉❉❉❉❉❉❉❉❉❉❉❉❉❉

BARRY MASON

Barry Mason is a prolific songwriter. He is also one of my best friends. He wrote the lyrics to lots of hits. A great deal were cowritten with Les Reed who wrote the music.

They wrote several songs for a show called *"Les Bicyclettes de Belsize"*. After a period of very hard cerebral work, they were pleased to have completed the project.

Then came the bombshell. Where was the title song? They told the producer that the title *"Les Bicyclettes de Belsize"* didn't exactly roll off the tongue.

The producer was adamant that a title song must be written. So, back to work, Barry and Les. They eventually composed the title song and unbelievably, it was the one and only hit song of the project. It was recorded by Engelbert Humperdinck.

Barry tells this story against himself. He was in a public toilet spending a penny.

In the stall next to him was a chap who was whistling one of Barry's hits *"Delilah"*.

Barry couldn't resist telling the chap that he wrote that song.

The chap asked if Barry wrote the words or the music. Barry told him that he had written the words. The chap said to Barry "I wasn't whistling the words."

What a deflater!

Barry and I have written several songs together. Sadly, thirty years too late, but we had fun. We used to meet at my house and write unsuccessfully but enjoyed each other's company.

Again I have to tell you that he has died since I wrote this epistle. He left us with Happy Memories and I miss him.

❉❉❉❉❉❉❉❉❉❉❉❉❉❉❉❉❉

TONY HATCH

Tony Hatch was and still is a prolific composer. With his wife, Jackie Trent, he composed lots of commercial hit songs. He wrote a lot of his songs for Petula Clarke.

These songs were arranged for Pet by the great Johnny Harris who was with me in the Cyril Stapleton days. I was the pianist on most of the recordings.

In those days the artist usually put their voice on the record at a later date. Often with edits, so that the recording was immaculate.

I only found out who the artist was because I remembered the tune that I had played on.

Strange days, but most interesting.

✳✳✳✳✳✳✳✳✳✳✳✳✳✳✳✳✳✳

JOHNNY MERCER

Performing Songwriter

Johnny Mercer, 18 November 1909 – 25 June 1976.

Johnny Mercer was the most prolific songwriter of the popular American songbook.

His hundreds of Standard songs are far too many to list, so if you want to know the titles just Google him and you will be amazed.

Johnny and his wife Ginger came for dinner at my house. Marion knew them from the USA and when they were over here she made contact and we invited them out to dinner.

A very pleasant evening culminated, as usual, by me playing the piano with Johnny singing some of his fantastic library of songs.

I called Sir Michael Parkinson up and suggested that he might like to come up the road to enjoy a sing song. He loves good music.

He said "It's bloody ten o'clock."

I agreed that it was rather late but Johnny Mercer and I were having a musical evening.

At the mention of Johnny Mercer he said "I'll be right up."

Sir Michael joined us and we had a memorable gathering and what a sing song.

Many years later, my wife Maryann and I had a holiday near Charleston, South Carolina, and visited Johnny's grave.

Each of his family have the title of one of his songs on their gravestones.

Very poignant.

"And The Angels Sing".

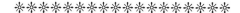

✳✳✳✳✳✳✳✳✳✳✳✳✳✳✳✳✳

Musicians

✳✳✳✳✳✳✳✳✳✳✳✳✳✳✳✳✳✳

MAYNARD FERGUSON

Maynard Ferguson had me really worried that he might explode.

He was a guest of the John Dankworth orchestra. We were doing a show at the Festival Hall in London. I was the pianist.

I don't think that Maynard was at his best and he was struggling to make those high screamers for which he was famous.

He had dug his own grave. He was expected to play notes that only dogs could hear.

What does he do when he is not feeling up to it? Well, to me, it looked as if he would explode.

I suppose that if you suck in a load of air and squash it, then the only way it comes out is very high or very low. He managed to be a freak, and all was well, but Maynard had me worried for a while.

Maynard Ferguson CM,
4 May 1928 – 23 August 2006.

Elsewhere.co.nz

✳✳✳✳✳✳✳✳✳✳✳✳✳✳✳✳✳✳

GEORGE KISH

George Kish came to England in 1956. He is Hungarian and there was a bit of trouble in Budapest which he preferred to get away from.

He played the fiddle. Now, violinists in England are not exactly of the same Gypsy-ish background as G Kish Esq. So George decided to learn the guitar. I think he spent a whole weekend learning it, then decided that he was ready for Soho.

I first met him in a seedy club (one of many I frequented in those days). He played very well considering he'd only had it in his hands for a couple of days. At the time I was working the Gargoyle Club. This was and still is a supper, dance, strip club.

The bandleader was Alan Kane. He needed a new guitar player so I recommended George. He was magnificent. If he didn't know the tune on guitar he'd get out the fiddle and give us a bit of the old Zigoina.

Many years later when I formed my quartet I asked George to be in it. We were together a long time, doing lots of broadcasts with Rolf Harris, and hundreds of late-night programmes.

George never really lost his Hungarianisms.

We were doing a Rolf Harris programme and in tea the break George mentioned that he was thinking of buying a new car.

He said that he liked the look of the Volvo. Taking the opportunity to take the Mickey out of him I asked if he had seen the Vauxhall Viva. In his magnificent innocence he replied that he had, but his Vife didn't like it!

❄❄❄❄❄❄❄❄❄❄❄❄❄❄❄❄❄❄❄

LARRY ADLER

Larry Adler was the greatest mouth organ player in the world. I know that is a fact because he told me so. Larry was not shy at coming forward. He dropped more names than I do.

I once did a George Gershwin concert in Jersey in the Channel Islands.

I accompanied Larry as he was the star of the evening.

He was a great raconteur, or name dropper. He had met everybody in Hollywood including Fred Astaire, Al Jolson and George Gershwin.

I played the Gershwin Preludes, which were quite difficult. After I had finished them, he came on stage and asked me to play the last one again.

He then played it with me, without music, perfectly. Clever clogs.

I once had dinner with him in a restaurant. When he saw the Maitre D' near us he took out a Dictaphone and made comments on the food. He pretended to be a restaurant critic.

It worked. The service and the food were elevated to first class.

He was of Russian stock. His parents name started with a Z so his father was always last in line to be called.

His father got wise and when he entered the USA he changed his name to Adler so that he was in the As.

Crafty old person, which ran in the family.

❄❄❄❄❄❄❄❄❄❄❄❄❄❄❄❄❄❄

With Barbara Windsor.

With Henry Cooper.

STEPHANE GRAPPELLI

Strangely, when one is associated with a legend it is not quite so stunningly impressive as it is after they have passed on.

Stéphane Grappelli, 26 January 1908 – 1 December 1997.

I imagine that it becomes more important to me because I realise that it can't be repeated.

"Nuages" was a tune composed by Stephane Grappelli and Django Rheinardt.

I never met Django but I was Stephane's pianist from 1961 until his death in December 1997, He was aged 89.

I met him because I was the pianist in the Cyril Stapleton orchestra and Stephane was a friend of Cyril.

The orchestra did a weekly television show called *The Melody Dances* from the Finsbury Park Empire.

Stephane was asked to be a guest artist on one of the shows and I played the piano for him.

We became firm friends and from then on we recorded many shows together.

We made 39 quarter hour broadcasts for Radio Luxembourg.

On one of them we recorded *"Route 66"* and Nelson Riddle came into the studio to hear it.

Twice on his birthdays I conducted the London Symphony Orchestra for him, playing my arrangements.

We quite often were called upon by the BBC to do the Jazz Club sessions.

I recorded five albums with him.

One was a Beatles-themed album which frankly didn't suit him at all.

One was called *Brandenburg Boogie* which was based on my arrangements of J S Bach's melodies.

I also played the piano on his albums with Yehudi Menuhin.

Big sellers, but not Stephane's cup of tea. Stephane played jazz ad lib while Yehudi played jazz written by Max Harris.

Chalk and cheese. Steph flowed and Yehudi played very stiffly.

Still, the albums sold very well. They first performed on the Michael Parkinson television show. Michael kick-started their success.

I remember that on one project Stephane was asked whether he would prefer an advance or a promise of future royalties.

He said, "I am 83, I'll have the money now."

Dear Stephane.

Some Photos
From My Album

My band on Parkinson.

With Liza Minnelli.

With Tony Blackburn.

With Cilla Black.

With Cliff Adams.

With Danny la Rue and my Band.

Some Male Actors (Some Who Sing)

❊❊❊❊❊❊❊❊❊❊❊❊❊❊❊❊❊❊❊

ALLAN SHERMAN

I was the musical director for the American singer and comedian, Allan Sherman.

We performed at the lovely Savoy theatre next to the Savoy hotel. The year was 1966.

After we had done two weeks at the Savoy theatre, he asked me to go with him to Germany, to perform at the united states bases there.

It was a wild time.

One night he asked me to go with him to an establishment of ill repute. I told him that I wasn't interested in that kind of activity, I had recently got married and was quite happy, thank you Allan. He said that he wanted my company, so I went with him.

While he was engaged in the chosen activity I sat and read a German newspaper, probably upside down, as I didn't know the

Allan Sherman, 30 November 1924 – 20 November 1973.

language. He eventually emerged with a contented smile on his face, and we went back to a fairly normal civilisation. He was a strange person, lonely obviously, yet we were pretty good friends.

When I needed a reference to work in the USA, I asked him for his help.

He signed a document that said that I was a reliable person and fit to work in the USA.

I never saw him again. Sad. Thank you Allan.

❊❊❊❊❊❊❊❊❊❊❊❊❊❊❊❊❊❊❊

JEREMY IRONS

In 1994 I was the musical director of the show to celebrate the 50th anniversary of the D-Day landings. Jeremy Irons was one of the guests. Some of the others were Bob Hope,

Vera Lynn, Anthony Newley and Mari Wilson.

Mr Irons was to sing "A Nightingale Sang In Berkeley Square".

I went to his house in leafy Berkshire Mr Irons was hospitable, nothing more.

To break the tense air I told him a humorous story about Elizabeth Taylor.

I wish I hadn't. No reaction.

Anyway, we rehearsed *"Nightingale"* and arranged to record it at Stringfellows Club in London.

On the day I had done the arrangement for my trio and Mr Irons came in and lit a cigarette and we proceeded to record.

Unfortunately, as he sang *"A Nightingale Sang In Berkeley Square"* the cigarette smoke went in his eyes … re-take.

He should have sung *"Smoke Gets In Your Eyes"*.

❄❄❄❄❄❄❄❄❄❄❄❄❄❄❄❄❄

HUGH GRIFFITHS

I was asked to help the famous actor Hugh Griffiths to sing a song as an audition for a film. I think it was *"If I Could Speak To The Animals"*, something like that. I was asked to meet him in a room which was over a pub. A drastic mistake!

He was not a very good singer and I believed that he didn't really want the part in the film anyway. So after about 15 minutes he suggested that we went downstairs for a drink.

It was about 11.15 in the morning. We drank all day.

In the evening we went to my flat where my wife cooked us something or other and of course we washed it down with wine. We were the best of friends for life! I took him home, no drink driving problems in those days, and we promised to continue our friendship for the rest of our lives.

We had had a wonderful boozy day. That was the last I saw of Hugh Griffiths.

We didn't keep in touch and I never saw him again!

❄❄❄❄❄❄❄❄❄❄❄❄❄❄❄❄❄

KIRK DOUGLAS

When I was 20 odd years old I saw a fantastic movie called *Spartacus*. It starred Kirk Douglas.

I became England's answer to Spartacus immediately. I was so impressed by his physique, strength and good looks. I was of course kidding myself.

Anyway, Kirk Douglas would be embedded in my psyche for ever. Many, many years later I was the musical director of the *Parkinson* television show.

When there was a self-contained musical group on the show I left the stage and sat in the "waiting to go on" room. I went in and sitting there alone was Kirk "Spartacus" Douglas.

In my dreams I would have shaken hands, introduced myself and told him how much I admired him, and told him of the influence he had on me so many years ago.

But, I was overawed and speechless!

I sat down and didn't even say hello to him.

After the musical group had finished their number I went back on stage.

I missed my chance to grovel with KIRK.

I will always regret it, silly me.

❄❄❄❄❄❄❄❄❄❄❄❄❄❄❄❄❄

ERNIE WISE

Ernie and Doreen Wise were neighbours of ours across the river, and good friends.

We often went to our favourite Chinese restaurant in Maidenhead which is sadly no longer there.

Also sadly no longer there, is Ernie. When he died there was a funeral service at Slough Crematorium.

One of Ernie's favourite songs was "The Shadow Of Your Smile".

Doreen asked if I would play it and asked our mutual friend, Teddy Johnson, to sing it.

It was an emotional moment.

At least we sent him off with a good song.

Google

Ernie Wise OBE,
27 November 1925 – 21 March 1999.

Doreen and I were an item for a while. We used to meet at her house in Dorney, have a glass of Champagne, and go to eat our favourite supper, fish and chips.

I don't think Ernie would mind as we were all good friends.

I suddenly realised that my future was with Maryann, so Doreen and I parted amicably. She has since joined Ernie in Heaven.

A good friend and a lovely lady.

Rest in Peace Doreen.

Some of My Musical Collaborations

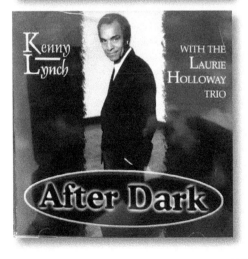

✳ ✳✳✳✳✳✳✳✳✳✳✳✳✳✳✳✳✳✳

Two Bandleaders and a Musical Polymath

✳✳✳✳✳✳✳✳✳✳✳✳✳✳✳✳✳✳✳

EDDIE MENDOZA

My first exciting engagement was at the Theatre Royal in my hometown of Oldham, Lancashire. Now sadly Greater Manchester.

I got home from school one day, I was 14 I think. I was alone because mum was working at the cotton mill and dad was French polishing somewhere.

The doorbell rang and confronting me was a whiskered gentleman who said he was Eddie Mendoza.

I used to go to a music shop and play the latest sheet music on their piano. I couldn't afford to buy all the top twenty so I used to go to the shop and learn to play it by memory.

Eddie Mendoza was appearing at the Theatre Royal that week with his band called The Crazy Loonies.

Apparently his pianist had not turned up or was in a ditch somewhere the worse for drink.

So Eddie had gone to the nearest music shop and asked if they knew of any available piano players.

They told Eddie about me and hence the knock on our door at 71 Trafalgar Street, Oldham.

I asked him what I should play and he said anything! Just look a bit stupid.

That was the easy bit. The rest of the group would be acting very stupidly while I played.

I left a note for mum and dad that I had gone to the Theatre Royal and I would be home later.

Eddie produced a tartan jacket that was far too big for me and a wig. I put them on and entered showbusiness.

At the end of the first performance I was pleased to see my parents who had been at the show because of my note.

The "Star" of the show and the producer was Roy Fransen. He did a high dive into a tank of water. Yes, truly. It was that kind of show.

I had a wonderful week.

I fell in love with the lady accordionist only to find out that she was spoken for, by a west country comedian called Benny Hill.

At the end of the week I was paid by cheque the gigantic sum of £5 by Roy Fransen.

I gave it to my father of course, It bounced!

Welcome to showbusiness.

Several weeks later we discovered that his act was appearing at Morecambe. We went there and confronted him with the bounced cheque. He apologised and said that he had been going through a hard time.

He ripped up the bounced cheque and gave us another one of the same value. Guess what! It bounced!

✳ ✳✳✳✳✳✳✳✳✳✳✳✳✳✳✳✳✳✳✳✳

Two Bandleaders and a Musical Polymath

✳✳✳✳✳✳✳✳✳✳✳✳✳✳✳✳✳✳✳✳

WOODY HERMAN

Thanks to Woody Herman I spent a week in Vancouver and never saw daylight.

I was playing the piano for my wife, Marion Montgomery, in a club in Chinatown. We did two sets and finished the performance about 1 am.

Woody's band was also in town. They were playing at some other club. When the band had finished, at about the same time as us, these young "thundering" and roaring players had not had enough release to be able to call it a night and go to bed.

Their pianist was the legendary Nat Pierce. He was one of the older members of the band.

When they had finished their show at about 1 am he had had enough and was ready to call it a day. That left the young tigers without a piano player.

Enter me!

We all assembled at another club and played all night until we dropped. Jazzed out.

The person I remember most of all was the band's lead trumpet player, Bill Chase. He carried on where Maynard Ferguson left off.

Very strong and exciting.

Sadly, in 1974 he died in a plane crash. That week, I was as happy as a pig in a *lot* of dirt.

All week, every night, just playing great music. Firstly with Marion, and then with the thundering herd of Woody Herman.

I therefore slept all day long.

I got out of bed and went to start the evening off with Marion and then to the blow with Woody's band. On the last night we played more than usual. When I went outside it was dawn.

The sunlight dazzled me and I saw that Vancouver was surrounded by beautiful mountains.

That was my Vancouver, for a few minutes, as I went back to my bed in the hotel.

The only time I saw or spoke to Woody Herman was many years earlier when I got his autograph, which I still have, when I was in New York doing my stint on the RMS Carinthia.

Thanks, Woody, for the use of your band!

✳✳✳✳✳✳✳✳✳✳✳✳

❄ ❄❄❄❄❄❄❄❄❄❄❄❄❄❄❄❄❄❄

Two Bandleaders and a Musical Polymath

❄❄❄❄❄❄❄❄❄❄❄❄❄❄❄❄❄❄❄❄

MEL TORME

At the aforementioned Cool Elephant sophisticated night club, we had the great Mel Tormé as the star guest for two weeks.

He was a great singer and I was very pleased to play the piano for him.

I remember that in one section of the show he always asked for requests.

Someone asked for a song and he told me that we would do that one.

Horrified I had to tell Mel that I didn't know the song.

He said "You will in a minute," and sang in a way that I could hear the chords, and we got through it without losing a beat.

Incidentally, David Frost was in the audience one night with his date, the beautiful Janette Scott.

Mel was invited to their table and immediately fell madly in love with Janette.

Mel Tormé, 13 September 1925 – 5 June 1999.

I don't know how he did it, but in no time he took her away from David and married her.

I have had the pleasure of playing piano for their son James. He uses Mel's arrangements that I played 50 years ago. More happy memories.

❄❄❄❄❄❄❄❄❄❄❄

✸ ✸✸✸✸✸✸✸✸✸✸✸✸✸✸✸✸✸✸✸

HRH Princess Margaret

✸✸✸✸✸✸✸✸✸✸✸✸✸✸✸✸✸✸✸

A DINNER PARTY

Princess Margaret, Countess of Snowdon,
CI, GCVO, GCStJ, CD,
21 August 1930 – 9 February 2002.

John Dankworth and Cleo Laine (Mrs Dankworth) had an annual lunch where the young musical stars of the day were presented with awards.

My wife, Marion, and I were invited to the lunch, at the Guildhall in Westminster. The guest of honour was Princess Margaret.

We were gathered in a circle ready to be introduced or greeted by the princess. She shook hands with the majority ofthe guests and occasionally pecked on the cheek the people that were her friends.

My adjacent guest whispered that the kissed people must be very well known to her. She got round to me and kissed me on the cheek. My adjacent friend nearly fell over with surprise.

Actually, some time before, she had confided in me that she didn't normally kiss men with a beard, but made an exception with me.

The evening before this particular lunch she had been given the guest list. She saw that I was taking my daughter Abigail as my wife Marion was away.

My phone rang and it was Princess Margaret. She asked if I would mind if Abigail sat with someone else and I would sit with her. I of course agreed.

We had a jolly time as we were of course sitting with John and Cleo. Lots of laughter and funny stories.

Confidentially she asked how I managed when Marion was away.

Enough said!

✸ PRAYERS ✸

Every Sunday in every church the congregation prays for the Queen. Princess Margaret wondered (to me) if that made the Queen feel better on Sundays.

NURSERY RHYMES

One day the phone rang and a gentleman said that Princess Margaret would like to talk to me. It actually was genuine but you never know with musicians. It could have been a friend having me on.

Anyway it was the real Princess Margaret. She asked me if I was free the next day,

and if so would I go to the palace and play the piano for the Queen and herself.

I told her that I was indeed free and which palace would I go to?

She said Buckingham Palace of course. She and the Queen had decided to record several nursery rhymes, which they had learned from their grandfather, as a present for the Queen mother's 90th birthday.

Wow!

I agreed of course and asked if I could prepare any music for the recording. She told me that I would know all the songs and gave me one title, "I Know Where The Flies Go In The Wintertime".

I immediately called the publisher and asked them to bike it down to me post haste.

The next day I arrived at the palace at 2.25 pm for a 2.30 pm meeting with the Queen and Princess Margaret.

I was met at the front door by a flustered gentleman who told me that lunch had finished early and that I was being awaited.

I had met the Queen a few times before, at Christmas parties at Kensington Palace.

But this was different of course.

I told Princess Margaret that she would be pleased that I had managed to get "I Know Where The Flies Go…". She looked at my only piece of music and told me that it was the wrong one!

The Queen told me that due to "that band" practising for some royal event, we had to use a different room which was quieter.

In the room was a grand piano, a recording engineer ("the one who does my speech at Christmas") and two microphones.

Also in the room were two ladies in waiting, one being Jean Wills who had been to my house previously with Princess Margaret.

So I suddenly became the musical director! I suggested (you don't tell the Queen) that they should sing each tune through, and I would assess the key, the chords and the routine. I suggested (again) that we recorded one piece at a time.

So off we went. I think we recorded about 14 tunes, none of which I had ever heard before.

At the end of this exciting afternoon we decided (they decided) to listen to what we (they) had done.

I noticed that Princess Margaret sat in the big chair while the Queen sat in a smaller one. Just an observation…

All had been recorded well and the result was a one-off birthday present for the Queen Mother.

The recording engineer, BBC I think, was told to make only one copy of the afternoon's singing.

If it got out the press would go berserk, hence only one copy.

I was dying for a cup of tea but none was offered.

I asked the Queen if the grandfather who taught them these nursery rhymes was King George the Fifth but she told me that it was the Queen Mother's father, the Earl of Strathmore.

❋❋❋❋❋❋❋❋❋❋❋❋❋❋❋❋❋❋

Sometime later, during a party at my house, Princess Margaret told me about the delivery of the tape for her mother's birthday.

It was given to the Queen Mother at "her house in Windsor". I believe that was Royal Lodge.

Apparently the two daughters gave the audio cassette to the Queen Mother and were told that as the Queen Mother didn't have the proper sound equipment, they would have to go and listen to it in the car outside.

This they did. It was a wonderfully successful birthday present.

Later that day Prince Charles turned up and wanted to listen to the now-famous recording.

He was told that he could listen to it but had to go outside to the car.

He then astounded everyone by opening a cupboard which contained the latest in sound equipment.

The Queen Mother was amazed that she had all that equipment but didn't know! She no longer had to sit in the car to listen to her two daughters singing for her.

❋❋❋❋❋❋❋❋❋❋❋❋❋❋❋❋❋❋

Queen goes on record

EXCLUSIVE by Clare Brotherwood

MUSICIAN Laurie Holloway has spoken about the time he accompanied the Queen and Princess Margaret as they recorded songs they had learned as children.

Laurie broke a 12-year silence about the recording sessions after it was revealed he was the only person who had recorded her singing.

In the south USA, the TV musical director, composer and pianist had been completely oblivious to the revelation until friends e-mailed him.

■ LAURIE HOLLOWAY

"I have kept quiet all these years and I am quite surprised that the Queen must have mentioned my name," he said from his holiday home in Georgia. "Now that it's out

I'm very pleased."

A long-time friend of Princess Margaret, who used to sing at parties Laurie and his wife, jazz singer Marion Montgomery, gave at their Bray home, the musician recalled: "It was for the Queen Mother's 90th birthday, I believe.

"Princess Margaret called me and asked if I was free the following day to go to the palace to help record and play the piano for the Queen and herself while they were singing songs they had learned as children from their grandfather, the Earl of Strathmore.

"When I got there the BBC had arranged to record it with two microphones and a tape recorder.

"I didn't have a clue what they were going to sing but I took over as musical director and suggested they sing each song unaccompanied so that I could find out what key they were singing in and also to learn the songs."

Laurie says he can't remember the songs except 'I Know Where Flies Go In Wintertime', when he had to stop as they sang 'bump, bump'.

As far as he knows, there was only one tape.

"We did about 16 tracks and when they took it to the Queen Mother's house in Windsor she did not know if she had a tape recorder. But later it was discovered that she had a whole set of hi-fi in a cupboard!"

Golden Jubilee special – pages 35 to 46

DINING OUT

We were often invited to Kensington Palace for evenings with Princess Margaret.

One night involved carol singing after dinner. At dinner I sat next to Colin Tennant, the chap who gave PM (as she was known intimately) the gift of a 10-acre plot of land on the island of Mustique, where she built a villa called Les Jolies Eaux.

After dinner we went into the main room to sing Christmas carols. The Queen joined us.

The choir was from Kensington church I believe.

As it was unaccompanied, they found the pitch of the carol from a pitch pipe. Each time they played the pipe Princess Margaret would move her hands indicating that she wanted it to be in a lower key.

At one point I heard the Queen say disappointedly that there was only Princess Margaret, Cleo Laine and Marion Montgomery singing with her.

Some backing group!

❄❄❄❄❄❄❄❄❄❄❄❄❄❄❄❄❄

Meeting Prince Charles.

TIMING

Princess Margaret was renowned to be a late night person. One evening I had booked my taxi for midnight, hoping that it wasn't too early. The party ended at 11pm!

I told our host the predicament.

So she said that I had better play the piano for everybody until the car arrived.

She was very kind, to me anyway.

❄❄❄❄❄❄❄❄❄❄❄❄❄❄❄❄❄

FRANK SINATRA

I was booked to play the piano on a concert with Frank Sinatra and I had arranged to take Princess Margaret to the rehearsal.

Soon after all this was arranged, Gordon Mills asked me to go to the USA as musical director for Engelbert Humperdinck. I said that I would love to go with Engelbert, but I had to return to play for Sinatra, who was one of my idols.

He asked if I was booked by the Harold Davison agency to play for Sinatra.

I told him that I was. He told me that I was relieved of the job as he had just bought the Harold Davison agency. My dream of playing for Sinatra had been thwarted.

I had to tell Princess Margaret that I was very sorry, but I had to take a rain check.

Which of course I did.

✳✳✳✳✳✳✳✳✳✳✳✳✳✳✳✳✳

INTRUSION

I was asked by Princess Margaret to organise a musical evening at the American ambassador's house in Regents Park, London.

The guests were Annie and Vince Hill, John and Cleo Dankworth and because he was in london, the fabulous trumpeter Clark Terry.

At one point Princess Margaret came up to me and wondered if I would mind asking "that trumpet player" to play a little quieter.

It takes all kinds. Of course I said yes to her but didn't dare, or want, to ask the great Clark to keep it down.

Ah well, another great memory, and still available to watch on YouTube.

✳✳✳✳✳✳✳✳✳✳✳✳✳✳✳✳✳

PHOTOGRAPHS

Most people with a piano have their family photos on top of the piano. I have my family on mine. So it was quite an eye opener when I played Princess Margaret's piano. The photos on top were of King George the 6th and the Queen Mother. The Queen and Prince Phillip. Princess Margaret's children David and Sarah.

Quite a heavy load of relations for me to stare at. Not easy to play jazz looking at those photos.

I should have played the National Anthem!

✳✳✳✳✳✳✳✳✳✳✳✳✳✳✳✳✳

My investiture with an MBE.

❊ ❊❊❊❊❊❊❊❊❊❊❊❊❊❊❊❊❊

Classical Orchestras

❊❊❊❊❊❊❊❊❊❊❊❊❊❊❊❊❊❊

I was a guest on the *Last Night of the Proms* with the BBC concert Orchestra on September the 11th 1999. It was compered by Terry Wogan and featured John Dankworth, Kiri te Kanawa, Evelyn Glennie, and my trio.

I played a Duke Ellington medley and accompanied Dame Kiri on something, I forget.

I was also the featured soloist with the Concert Orchestra on the radio programme *Friday Night is Music Night*. It was quite a day. Obviously a Friday. I decided to get the train rather than have a long drive.

The train approached Crewe and stopped. After a long time there was an announcement that the train driver had gone and his replacement hadn't turned up. I panicked.

The radio programme was live in Llandudno. I managed to get a taxi to take me all the way and I got there with very little time to spare. What a day it was. Not to be repeated, I hope.

The London Symphony Orchestra at the Barbican had a three day season called the *Summer Pops*. I was the musical director of the LSO and featured soloist for the three days. My guests were Cab Calloway, Barbara Cook, and Arturo Sandoval. It was good experience.

My usual guys have a way of playing a dotted quaver and a semiquaver as a triplet. The LSO play it as a dotted quaver and a semiquaver, as it is written. Not right for my arrangements. I had to write a lot of the arrangements in 12/8 so that the LSO would get the jazz feel.

It seemed to work.

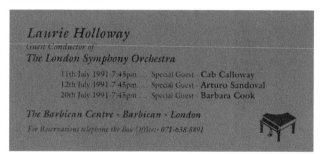

The three days were a gas, I enjoyed it very much, except when Arturo Sandoval's pianist forgot to bring on his music and I had to send him off to get it.

A good time was had by most of us. I remember Alec Firman at London Weekend Television educating me on conducting. I was trying to conduct with both of my hands. He advised me to put my left hand in my pocket.

Good advice for a novice like me.

I was asked by my friend Gilbert O'Sullivan to conduct the Irish Concert Orchestra for him in Dublin. I had done most of the arrangements so I knew what I was doing.

They enjoyed playing Gilbert's songs because it was different from their usual repertoire.

Gilbert and I also did a BBC radio broadcast in London with the BBC Concert Orchestra. Great fun. They were playing unusual stuff and we were working with classicists for a change.

Music is music, whoever is playing it.

✤ ✤✤✤✤✤✤✤✤✤✤✤✤✤✤✤✤

Marion

✤✤✤✤✤✤✤✤✤✤✤✤✤✤✤✤✤✤

Marion Montgomery, 17 November 1934 –22 July 2002.
Dudley Moore CBE, 19 April 1935 – 27 March 2002.

Marion and I had been going out for about 2 months, when we were married in the States on 16 June 1965. We had 37 happy years together.

My dear wife died a very sad and early death in 2002. A non-smoker, passive smoking from singing in the clubs had caused her to contract lung cancer.

✤✤✤✤✤✤✤✤✤✤✤✤✤✤✤✤✤

MARION MONTGOMERY ALBUMS

Marion In The Morning
For The Love Of Mercer Volume 1
For The Love Of Mercer Volume 2
That Lady From Natchez
Mellow
Sometimes In The Night
I Gotta Right To Sing / Nice And Easy
(double cd)
Skylark
Ballads And Blues
Makin' Whoopee
What's New
At Ronnie Scott's

✳ ✳✳✳✳✳✳✳✳✳✳✳✳✳✳✳✳✳✳

From One Subject To Another

✳✳✳✳✳✳✳✳✳✳✳✳✳✳✳✳✳✳✳

RAY BROWN

Discogs

Ray Brown, October 13, 1926 – July 2, 2002.

Ray Brown was the fantastic bass player with pianist Oscar Peterson and they were in London doing concerts.

I was working at a drinking den called the 142 Charing Cross Road with the bass player Joe Mudele and the bandleader Johnny Gray. Ray Brown was a friend of Joe Mudele and came to the club to say hello.

It was our interval and we had a very nice chat. Ray had at one time been married to the great Ella Fitzgerald.

Then Johnny, the bandleader, said that it was time to go back to work. I started to play the piano which was facing the wall and suddenly I was musically lifted to new heights, Ray Brown was playing the bass.

No discredit to Joe Mudele but wow, what a difference.

It almost explained why Oscar was so good.

But in his favour, Joe introduced me to the game of golf. Joe was married to Rose.

They were driving past a lake one day and Rose commented on the lovely view. Joe said that it was about a seven iron. He said that was the beginning of the end of their marriage.

Good old Joe.

✳✳✳✳✳✳✳✳✳✳✳✳✳✳✳✳✳✳

JOHN AND CLEO AGAIN

John Dankworth once offered me his house for £1,000 less than the price that he was offered. We were in Monte Carlo at the Sporting Club. I was playing the piano for Cleo and after the performance we were invited to an upmarket party.

Cleo and Marion were whisked away to the dance floor by upper crusters and John and I sat and chatted because we weren't dancers.

John and Cleo were about to sell their lovely house in Aspley Guise near Woburn.

They had found a bigger and better house nearby and decided to sell and move.

John really loved the house and to keep it in the family he told me that when he had a firm offer he would let me have it for £1,000 less than the offer.

I didn't take him up mainly because I didn't have £1,000 in the first place.

Later, Cleo went solo and, as already mentioned, I was her pianist. We performed a recital format. The rhythm section was Ken Baldock on bass and Allan Ganley on drums. The leader was of course John Dankworth.

We would open the show with an instrumental and then Cleo would join us.

She had a repertoire which included Noel Coward, Schubert, Kurt Weil, Richard Rodney Bennet and John Dankworth.

One especially difficult piece for me was Don Banks' *"Settings From Roget"*.

I was at their house and John told me that the piece was on the piano. The line up was voice, saxophone, bass, drums and piano including 2 rubber plugs and an eraser.

It was a bewildering piece and I thought that the plugs were for my ears and the eraser was there to rub out as much as possible.

The plugs were in fact for preparing the strings in the piano which I marked with silver paper. This was alright until one evening the piano was tuned in between the rehearsal and the concert and the silver paper had been removed.

We got through the piece without mishap because a couple of wrong notes in a piece like that were not noticed.

After that I always did a quick check before we went on.

With Cleo Laine at various points in our careers.

❄ ❄❄❄❄❄❄❄❄❄❄❄❄❄❄❄❄❄

This Is Your Life

❄❄❄❄❄❄❄❄❄❄❄❄❄❄❄❄❄❄❄

Being musical director of the *Parkinson* show, on one occasion I had arranged to meet friends for a drink after the show was finished.

I turned around and saw, not Alistair McGowan, but Michael Aspel...

The friends didn't tell me about the upcoming surprise.

The show finished and the producer, who I think was Stuart Macdonald, said in my earphones that we had to redo a play on for Alistair McGowan.

I told the orchestra and waited for the cue.

Stuart said "cue the music" and suddenly the audience went berserk.

I turned around and saw, not Alistair McGowan but Michael Aspel coming down the staircase with his famous red book.

And so I was "red-booked". *This Is Your Life Laurie Holloway*, during Series 40 on Monday 20 March 2000.

I honestly didn't expect that honour because I had always been an accompanist, not an out-front person.

But the deed was done and I was whisked off to Teddington where Thames Television studios were.

At the time I was "on the wagon" and they put me in a dressing room full of superb sandwiches and Champagne.

I am rather pleased that I didn't touch the booze and stayed in control of the forthcoming events.

I was told that I could remain seated or stand for each guest. I decided to greet them by standing.

On one side were family and the other side were people that I had worked with over the years, and there was room for the incoming surprises.

The big ending was the super surprise, organised by my family and the production.

It was my first bandleader, Sid Willmot, and his wife. Some surprise!

When I was 17 years old he had fired me on New Year's Eve.

In the past he had a piano player/ drinking partner who had gone sick, that's why I got the job. When his drinking partner had recovered he was invited back and I was fired. Some surprise!

I could have punched him on the nose, but I didn't do that.

I pretended I was pleased to see him and so there was a happy ending to the programme.

I have the Big Red Book, somewhere.

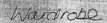
Wardrobe

THIS IS YOUR LIFE
FINGERS - L9876
GUEST LIST

Thursday 17th February

Surprise:	20.45
Rehearsal:	19.00 & 21.30 with Michael (Joining after the surprise)
Record:	23.00

Studio:	1
Green Rooms:	1

Production Office: 2nd Floor

Dressing Rooms: Michael: *209 - xtn: 2421*
Subject: *62 - xtn: 2028 or 2951*

Jackie & Jen Allen & Janet Keen : *Dressing Room 4 & 5*
(Des' Dress Room) - xtn: 2015

Elaine Paige: *101 xtn: 2405*
John Prescott: *108 xtn: 2013*

Warm Up: *207*

Other Guests: *102,103,104 & 105*

1ST REHEARSAL

NAME		ARRIVAL	
Jackie Allen	Walk On Spot V/O	18.45	Kilroy Cars
Jen Allen	On Set	18.45	Kilroy Cars
Charlie Aspinall	On Set Speaking	18.45	Kilroy Cars
John Harvey	On Set	18.45	Kilroy Cars
Abigail Hellens	Walk On Spot	18.45	Kilroy Cars
Mike Hellens	On Set	18.45	Kilroy Cars
Alice Holloway	On Set	18.45	Kilroy Cars
Karen Holloway	Walk On Spot	18.45	Driving

Production sheets for this episode alone ran to five pages of names, all
requiring either transport or an agreement as to how they were to get to
the studio and in which order. Two rehearsals were required
immediately prior to the televised event.

✳ ✳✳✳✳✳✳✳✳✳✳✳✳✳✳✳✳✳

Recognition, Compositions, Publishing and Recordings

✳✳✳✳✳✳✳✳✳✳✳✳✳✳✳✳✳✳

The British Academy
of Songwriters,
Composers and Authors,
trading as the Ivors
Academy, awarded
Marion and I their
gold badge for our
contributions to
British music.
A number of our
acquaintances were
also awarded that year.

At the 1993 Awards
the following are to be awarded a
Gold Badge of Merit

Norman Wisdom
John Nice
Elaine Page
Peter Foss
Denny Dennis
Russ Conway
Phil Kelsall
Geoffrey Emerick
Phyllis Rounce
Geoffrey Everett
David Wellsby
Nat Temple
John Peel
Laurie Holloway & Marion Montgomery
Roy Castle

Music

Brian Dee . . . Piano/Keyboards, Andy Grossart . . . Bass, Robin Hunt . . . Drums

SAXOPHONE AND CLARINET QUARTETS AND OTHERS

The Other Side of the Moon (alto saxophone and piano) commissioned for Erich Fackert. Published by Spartan Press.

Britannia Rag for saxophone quartet. Published by Spartan Press

Britannia Rag for solo piano and piano duet (unpublished).

Birdcall for saxophone quartet. Published by Spartan Press.

Running Buffet for saxophone quartet. Published by Spartan Press.

Jazz Suite for Bb clarinet and piano. Published by JustFlutes.

Joie de Vivre for clarinet quartet. Published by Spartan Press.

The Shoot for brass band. Published by Paxton.

Piano Trio Number 1 (unpublished).

Piano Trio Number 2 (unpublished).

Table and Private Room Reservations
FLE 6864   CIT 7405

Wig and Pen Club
230 STRAND, LONDON, W.C.2
Opposite Royal Court of Justice

WIG & PEN CLUB
229/230 STRAND, LONDON, W.C.2

The Wig & Pen club was formed in around 1908, with members drawn from lawyers, journalists and businessmen. It sadly closed in 2003.

I was nominated for membership by the Countess Pamela Juvenile and Shaw Taylor, the noted compere of the TV series *Police 5*.

❋❋❋❋❋❋❋❋❋❋❋❋❋❋❋❋❋❋

PUBLISHED MUSIC

I have written several pieces of music that have been published.

I had a friend, Michael Easton, who worked for Novello's music publishers.

The first music book was called *Pop Preludes* which was written for fairly easy piano.

One of the titles was "Walking Fingers" which was chosen as a test piece by the Royal School of Music.

Many others followed.

More Pop Preludes and lots for saxophone quartets and Clarinet quartets.

I wrote a piano suite which was a commission for the Young Pianist of the Year.

It was played on one of my concerts by my friend and classical pianist Brent Runnels, a distant relation.

I have composed a lot of signature tunes for television, but you've already read a bit about those.

RECORD ALBUMS

Showtime

About Time

Strictly Come Dancing

The Piano Player

Blue Skies

25 Golden Greats

Greatest Piano Hits

Fiddler On The Piano

Good Time

Cumulus

Brandenburg Boogie
(with Stephane Grappelli and Elena Duran)

Norwegian Wood

Live At Abbey Road

Then And Now

At The Piano

Bach To The Beatles

Laurie Holloway Solo

Happy Memories
(with Tina May)

After Dark
(with Kenny Lynch)

✳ ✳✳✳✳✳✳✳✳✳✳✳✳✳✳✳✳✳✳

Maryann

✳✳✳✳✳✳✳✳✳✳✳✳✳✳✳✳✳✳✳

Maryann and her husband were neighbours of Marion and myself. We often met for dinner. Maryann is a retired nurse.

My dear wife Marion developed cancer, seriously. She suffered bravely but she was losing the battle.

Ex-nurse Maryann looked after Marion and helped her enormously.

Marion bravely lost her battle in 2002. I was a widower but I was busy making music so that helped.

Maryann was divorced from her husband and was no longer my neighbour but lived in various rented flats in the area.

She and I eventually started dating as we had so much joint history. Things developed, we fell in love and married in Bray church in 2014.

My life is complete once more. I now have two families.

There are five grandsons. Three by my daughter Abigail, they are Freddie, Henry and Alfie, and two step-grandchildren by Lucinda, Maryann's daughter and her husband Myles in the USA. Those two boys are Sebastian and Benjamin.

I love them all.

I have also gained a step-son Peter, Maryann's son, and a step-daughter Karen, Peter's wife.

My other daughter is Karon who I adore.

I have been lucky to find Maryann and my step family.

Lucky person me, the piano player.

✳✳✳✳✳✳✳✳✳✳✳✳✳✳✳✳✳✳✳

Maryann and me on our wedding day in 2014...

... and on our honeymoon.

And Finally -
My Family Photos

Left: 95 year old brother, Marcus, and 15 yo grandson Alfie;

Above:my daughter Karon.

Below: Abigail, Freddie, Alfie and Henry,

My step-Irish family – Karen, left, with Aideen, Janet and Pat. Karen is married to Peter who is Maryann's son.

In America

Above: Maryann's daughter, Lucinda, with her husband Myles

Right: Sebastian and Benjamin.

"April In Paris"

THE CHANGING FACE OF WORK OVER THE DECADES, EACH APRIL

1956, APRIL

4	Extra gig	Queens Hotel, £2.5.0.
10	Extra gig	Royal Hotel.

1966, APRIL

2+3	Royal Festival Hall	John Dankworth + Royal Philharmonic Orch.
4	Playhouse	
5	Advision	
	Pye	
6	Maida Vale	Swing into Summer 8-13
8-13	Stockholm with Marion	
14	Broadcasting House	Saturday Swings, Aeolian
16	Marquee Jazz Club	Tony Kinsey
19	Manchester	Scene at 6.30 (Michael Parkinson)
22	Sydney, Australia	Bernstein Private party
25	Maida Vale	Prob. Music While You Work
26	Pye	
28	Elstree	Demo of TV Ident
	Broadcasting House	Saturday Swings

1976, APRIL

09	Sid Margo (fixer)	CTS, Macdonalds
12	Zodiac (Dean St)	French songs
27	Marion Montgomery	Birmingham Engine House
30	Sid Margo	John Wood studio, Young & Rubicam

1986, APRIL

08	Sid Margo	CBS, Dempsey & Makepeace
9	BBC	Maida Vale, M Montgomery
14	Tonia Davall	Lansdowne, Jose Maria
28	Sid Margo	CBS, Dempsey & Makepeace

1996, APRIL

3	Filming	Temple Golf Club Hole Number 5
3	Laurie & Marion	Routining Mercer project
4	Temple music evening	Skaila Kanga (harp) and Tommy Reilly
5	St Michaels church	
7	St Lukes church	
11	Rehearsal	Lily Savage (Paul O'Grady)
12	Rehearsal	Lily Savage and Barbara Dickson
14	Lily Savage TV show	Richard Drewett producer
19	Marion Montomgery	City Varieties Leeds
24	EMI	Jonathon Tunick session
27	Marion Montgomery	Newcastle

2002, APRIL

3	Laurie & Marion	Pizza on the Park, Paul Morgan, Harold Fisher
4	Parkinson TV series	S Johnston, J Culshaw, E Holmes
4	Marion Montgomery	Pizza on the Park
5	Laurie & Marion	Pizza on the Park
6	Laurie & Marion	Pizza on the Park
7	Marion Montomgery	LBC chat
8	Rehearse Marion's cruise trio	M Edmonstone, T Mark, J Jackson
11	Parkinson TV series	J Nesbitt, J Bridges, T Bennett
11	Laurie & Marion	Pizza on the Park
12	Laurie & Marion	Pizza on the Park
13	LH and Michael Parkinson	Oldham FC, Wycombe
13	Laurie & Marion	Pizza on the Park
18	Parkinson TV series	B Ferry, R Malo, C Tarrant, R Bryden, T Spall
18	Laurie & Marion	Pizza on the Park
19	Laurie & Marion	Pizza on the Park
20	Laurie & Marion	Pizza on the Park
22	Laurie & Kenny Lynch	Royal Oak, Dave Olney, Martin Drew
25	Parkinson TV series	J Tarbuck, M Collins, M Clunes

2011, APRIL

5	Pizza Express	Becki, J Jackson, H Fisher
6	Pizza Express	Barry Mason and my trio
7	Pizza Express	Kenny Lynch and my trio
8	Oxfordshire Golf Club	LH trio and Kenny Lynch
14	BBC Radio Berkshire	Interview with Henry Kelly
17	Cobham	LH trio and Kenny Lynch
28	Maidenhead Advertiser	Interview

Lightning Source UK Ltd.
Milton Keynes UK
UKHW051312010822
406663UK00006B/145